CONVERSING
with GOD *in* LENT

PRAYING THE SUNDAY MASS READINGS

WITH *LECTIO DIVINA*

CONVERSING *with* GOD *in* LENT

PRAYING THE SUNDAY MASS READINGS
WITH *LECTIO DIVINA*

STEPHEN J. BINZ

the WORD among us® Press

Published by The Word Among Us Press
9639 Doctor Perry Road
Ijamsville, Maryland 21754
wau.org

14 13 12 11 10   3 4 5 6 7

ISBN: 978-1-59325-165-9

Cover design by DesignWorks

Made and printed in the United States of America.

Library of Congress Cataloging-in-Publication Data

Binz, Stephen J., 1955-
Conversing with God in Lent : praying the Sunday Mass readings with lectio divina / Stephen J. Binz.
    p. cm.
Includes bibliographical reference (p.   ).
ISBN 978-1-59325-165-9 (alk. paper)
1. Lent--Prayers and devotions. 2. Catholic Church--Prayers and devotions. 3. Bible--Devotional literature. 4. Catholic Church. Lectionary for Mass (U.S.) I. Title.
BX2170.L4B56 2010
242'.34--dc22
                                        2009044786

Dedicated to
George Martin
Mentor and Friend

Founding editor and publisher
of *God's Word Today* magazine,
who taught me the sacred art of
reading Scripture as the word of God

Contents

Preface

In my previous book, *Conversing with God in Scripture: A Contemporary Approach to Lectio Divina*, I pondered the tradition of lectio divina and explored ways in which this ancient art could be cultivated by people in our day. I reflected on the movements—lectio, meditatio, oratio, contemplatio, and operatio—and suggested ways that readers might incorporate lectio divina into their lives as disciples. I concluded with a few examples of how selected passages of Scripture could be taken up in lectio divina and lead the reader to interior transformation.

Since the publication of that book, interest in lectio divina has continued to grow, not only in its seedbed within the Catholic and Orthodox traditions, but in Protestant and Evangelical communities as well. Christians everywhere are rediscovering the rich potential of this ancient practice. The worldwide Synod of Bishops and the recent teachings of Pope Benedict XVI have encouraged lectio divina for all the people of God.

A favorable response to my first book prompted The Word Among Us Press to ask me to continue this ancient yet contemporary approach to lectio divina with the Lectionary readings of the Lenten season. What follows is a consideration of the tradition of lectio divina during Lent and an exposition of the Sunday readings of the Lectionary based on the five established movements of the practice.

As in the previous book, I have created a work that can be used either privately or in groups. Individuals may use this for their own Lenten practice, or churches and communities may wish to incorporate this work into their Lenten journey together. It is also written with the catechumenal community in mind, since a prayerful reflection on the Lectionary of Lent is one of the most ancient forms of spiritual growth for the Elect who are preparing to enter the church and celebrate the Easter mysteries.

How To Use This Book

If you choose to use this book for your own personal growth during this season, simply spend some quiet time during each week of Lent with the Scriptures of the upcoming Sunday. The five movements of lectio divina will guide you through the reflective process. Led by the Holy Spirit, you can expect to be changed and renewed by God's living word through this ancient practice. Realize this book is only a guide, and that you should feel free to follow as many or as few of the suggestions as you choose. Do not think, for example, that you must meditate on each of the questions provided. You will be led to reflect on whatever God's Spirit brings to your mind and heart after each Scripture.

If you choose to follow this book with a small group, you will reap the wisdom and support of others, which can be an enormous help in experiencing the transforming power of Scripture (see the chapter "Collatio: Forming Community Through Scripture" from my previous book). Groups should meet once a week during Lent to reflect together on the Scriptures for the upcoming Sunday, or they may meet immediately after the Mass to continue the prayerful listening to that Sunday's readings. Members should read the first two chapters of this book in advance, and if they wish, may reflect on the questions of the meditatio at home before coming to the group. A facilitator guides the group through each step of lectio divina, honoring each movement with the attention it requires. Most of the discussion will center on the questions of the meditatio, but the group should feel free to decide which questions to consider and should not be compelled to discuss them all.

This work would also be an ideal way for the whole parish to enter into prayerful unity with the catechumens and candidates of the parish during Lent. The Elect and those called to continuing conversion may use this book as they are sent forth from the Lenten liturgy to reflect more deeply on the word of God. The rest of the community may follow this lectio divina on the same Scriptures, either individually or in small groups, during the week.

As you ponder the perennial question this year, "What are you going to do for Lent?" I invite you not just to give something up but to take something up as well. Take up the time-honored practice of lectio divina during this season and savor its grace.

Stephen J. Binz

Chapter One

Prayerfully Listening to God's Word during Lent

L ent is the ideal season for the practice of lectio divina. As the darkness of winter gives way to the light of spring, we spend forty days in the process of conversion, turning our hearts away from sin and toward the light of Christ. Through our practice of this ancient art, the seed of God's word begins to sprout and leaf through lectio and meditatio. With attentive reflection, the living word then buds and blossoms in oratio and contemplatio. Finally, the fruit of the Spirit begins to show forth in operatio as the harvest of the word of God.

The goal of our Lenten practices is the deepening of our longing for God as we prepare to celebrate the great mysteries that are at the heart of the Christian faith. This interior longing for God is the source of real prayer, and lectio divina cultivates that deep desire as we wait for Easter. Perhaps Lent teaches us, above all, that a Christian is not so much someone who does things for God but someone who deeply realizes, like Mary, that "the Mighty One has done great things for me" (Luke 1:49).

Both Lent and lectio divina seek to incorporate within the believer the reality of God's loving initiative. During Lent we deepen our desire to accept the new life that God has given us in Christ. When our longing is intense and our thirst for God is strong, we can receive God's gifts with appreciative joy. Lectio divina shows us how to approach Scripture with a receptive and expectant spirit. We open our hearts to God's initiative and listen carefully for the gifts of truth God offers us there. As St. Bernard of Clairvaux said, "The thirsty soul eagerly prolongs its contact with Scripture, certain to find there the One for whom it thirsts."[1]

When we pray using lectio divina during the season of Lent, we realize that we practice it not so much in order to do something for God but rather to open our hearts to the greatest gift God offers us—the life, death, and resurrection of his Son, Jesus. Lectio divina teaches us to first listen and receive, and only then respond. Our Christian lives become, then, a response to the love that God has first shown us in Christ—and a continual openness to his initiative, the grace he is offering us at every moment of our lives.

A Call to Fasting, Prayer, and Almsgiving

The season of Lent begins with the Scriptures' clarion call to return to God with our whole heart. In the Lectionary text for the Ash Wednesday liturgy, the prophet Joel decrees, "Blow the trumpet in Zion! / Proclaim a fast, / call an assembly. / Gather the people, / notify the congregation" (2:15-16). The time for repentance and conversion of heart is at hand. This is not private advice, but a pronouncement for all God's people. "Rend your hearts, not your garments, and return to the LORD, your God" (Joel 2:13).

The purpose of fasting, as the biblical tradition asserts, is not to get something from God or do something for God. Fasting, or any Lenten practices in which we deprive ourselves of life's usual stuff, is meant to deepen our inner longing for God's word. Joel

1 Bernard of Clairvaux, *Sermons on the Canticle of Canticles*, 23, n. 3: *Patrologia Latina* 183, 885d.

announced a fast within the assembly of God's people because Israel had lost the experience of God's presence among them. Fasting was their response to the grief of turning away from God and their repentance for the injustices they had committed. God's people fasted as their reaction to the moment in which they felt they must earnestly seek God again. As we respond to the call of the prophet, fasting helps us to take on a receptive spirit, to open our hearts to God, to hunger and thirst for his presence.

The somber chant of the Miserere (Psalm 51) on Ash Wednesday instills within us the spirit of this season of repentance:

> A clean heart create for me, O God,
>   and a steadfast spirit renew within me.
> Cast me not out from your presence,
>   and your holy spirit take not from me.
> Give me back the joy of your salvation,
>   and a willing spirit sustain in me. (verses 12-14)

We pray for the kind of interior renewal that only God's grace can provide. God's creative power can remake our hearts and give us back a spirit that longs for God's presence and the joy of God's salvation. This is the spirit of Lent, the spirit that lectio divina encourages within us. The season is not about giving up something for God, but about desiring God again, so that he may remake our hearts.

We often think of Lent in terms of self-inflicted suffering and glum acts of penance. But a persistent spirit of sadness and gloominess is not a Christian one. In the gospel reading for Ash Wednesday, Jesus urges us to fast without glumness, to pray without vanity, and to give alms without smugness (Matthew 6:1-6, 16-18). Jesus advocates these traditional practices of Lent not so that we will receive a reward from God or praise from anyone else. Fasting, prayer, and almsgiving, as encouraged by Jesus, are ways of seeking God and responding to his presence.

The practice of lectio divina can purify these disciplines within us. Fasting can help keep our spirits uncluttered by the concerns of the world and more sensitive to listening to God's voice in Scripture. Prayer behind closed doors can cultivate the quiet focus and purity of heart so necessary for reflective meditation on God's word. Almsgiving without others noticing it becomes a contemplative response of a transformed heart, which is the result of lectio divina.

The Baptismal and Penitential Focus of Lent

The restoration of the catechumenate and its Lenten rituals has reemphasized for the church the original baptismal character of Lent. The forty-day season evolved in the early church as a period of intense preparation for the sacraments of Christian initiation to be celebrated at Easter. Following the Rite of Election on the First Sunday of Lent, those preparing for baptism enter into the period of purification and enlightenment. During this period, these Elect focus on the Sunday Lectionary, particularly the Cycle A readings, which were chosen with the themes of continuing conversion in mind.

On the Third, Fourth, and Fifth Sundays of Lent, the liturgy includes the Scrutinies, which are special prayers "to uncover, then heal all that is weak, defective, or sinful in the hearts of the elect; to bring out, then strengthen all that is upright, strong, and good"

(Rite of Christian Initiation of Adults, 141). The Elect are then dismissed from the assembly before the Liturgy of the Eucharist to continue their reflection and prayer over the Sunday Scriptures of Lent with their sponsors. Throughout this period, the Elect are invited to join with the whole church in the practice of fasting, deeper prayer, and works of charity.

The renewed catechumenal process is about the whole person—the intellectual, affective, and behavioral aspects of discipleship. It is not simply education for the mind; it involves a change of heart and a whole new way of life. During the Lenten period of purification and enlightenment, the emphasis is on a more intense spiritual preparation, consisting more in interior reflection than in catechetical instruction.

This return to Lent's original focus involves the whole church, as God's people support and encourage those preparing for baptism and as we prepare to renew our own baptismal commitment. An effort to practice lectio divina during Lent can help renew our Lenten disciplines and integrate them into this renewed perspective. Since the Sunday Scriptures of Lent originally evolved within the perspective of purification and conversion as part of the process of Christian initiation, reflective prayer with these texts can help focus the church's catholic imagination around the heart of Lent.

A secondary but related characteristic of the season of Lent originated with the penitential discipline of the early church. The Order of Penitents was modeled on the catechumenate and formed a process of second conversion for those who had fallen back into serious sin after baptism, especially those who had denied or betrayed the faith during times of persecution. Those who had sinned were expected to perform acts of penance during Lent in preparation for being received back into the fellowship of the church. The penitents were received back into the community during Holy Week, in time to celebrate the Easter mysteries once more with the Elect and with all the faithful.

Both the baptismal and penitential themes of Lent penetrate the Sunday Scriptures of these six weeks. Very early in the church's history, Lent became a time for all Christians to walk with those preparing for baptism and with those preparing to be received back into the church. With support, encouragement, and prayer, the faithful accompanied them on their journey and at the same time prepared to renew their own baptismal vows at Easter.

Today these same texts of Scripture invite the whole community to an ongoing conversion of heart and the continual transformation that the Christian life requires. Lectio divina is the process of prayerfully listening and meditating on these texts, united in the same Spirit as the early Christians. Returning to the heart of Lent and focusing on these ancient Scriptures of the church through lectio divina can reinvigorate these forty days with their seminal power.

The Cross Unveils Scripture as the Revelation of Christ

From the ashen sign on the forehead of Ash Wednesday to the wooden cross of Good Friday, the forty days keep us focused on the cross of Christ. We begin Lent with the rough and gritty marking, accompanied by the stark words of Genesis 3:19: "Remember you are dust and to dust you will return" or those demanding words, "Repent and believe in the gospel." The season comes to its solemn climax with the plaintive chant "Behold the wood of the Cross on which hung the Savior of the world." The cross accompanies our Lenten pilgrimage as we journey with Christ from the desert toward the hill of Calvary.

Planted on mountaintops around the world, mounted in church sanctuaries, displayed in Christian homes, and worn around the necks of believers, the cross is the primal symbol that most galvanizes the followers of Jesus. The cross is our symbol of tragedy as well as triumph. As the world's most hated instrument of torture, it expresses pain, betrayal, abandonment, and death. Yet the cross is also the figure of humanity's greatest hope—that suffering and death do not have the last word, that God is eternally faithful and trustworthy.

The beautiful motto of the Carthusian order is *Stat crux dum volvitur orbis*— "The cross is steady while the world is turning." As the sturdy spiritual fulcrum of the spinning world, the cross is the center of the Christian's Lenten contemplation. Attentive listening to the Scriptures of Lent, with the cross of Jesus as our constant focal point, can keep our lives stable in faith despite the confusion, allure, and frenzy of the world.

The cross is also at the center of Scripture. Since the whole Bible finds its ultimate meaning in the tragic and triumphant cross of Christ, the countless diverse fragments of scriptural texts take their place around that cruciform focal point of salvation history. All of Scripture leads to the cross, finds its final significance there, and comes to us for our meditation and prayer marked with the sign of the cross.

The Passion accounts tell us that at the death of Jesus on the cross, the curtain of the Temple was split from top to bottom. The veil that concealed the presence of God in mysterious darkness was torn open, revealing for all the way to God. Likewise, God's hidden plan for the world's redemption, concealed for ages within all the texts of Scripture, was unveiled through Christ's self-offering to the Father. Through the cross, the Holy Spirit opens the eyes and hearts of God's people so they can experience the Scriptures as the living word and the way to life.

Lent in the Way of Saint Benedict

St. Benedict, the foremost proponent of lectio divina in the Western church, suggests that Lent is the season to concentrate on this sacred reading of holy Scripture. In fact, in his *Rule*, Benedict goes so far as to rearrange the daily timetable of the monks so as to provide more time for lectio divina during these six weeks. By changing the monastic routine, he urges upon his monks a revitalized rhythm of life during the Lenten season.

But more important than the external schedule of Lent, Benedict considers the internal spirit of the monks during this season. In chapter 49 of his *Rule*, Benedict urges the members of the community to improve the quality of their spiritual lives during Lent and to consider what is lacking in their discipleship. For Benedict, as for other great spiritual masters, Lent is not about somber asceticism. Though he requires abstinence from food, drink, and other normal activities, he is more concerned with replacing what is missing in life or bringing back into focus what has become fuzzy and distorted. Benedict writes: "Therefore we urge that all in the monastery during these holy days of Lent should look carefully at the integrity of their lives and get rid in this holy season of any thoughtless compromises that may have crept in at other times" (*Rule of Benedict*, 49, paraphrased).

For Benedict and the church, Lent is a time to look closely at our lives and to renew our efforts to be what we say we want to be. It is the season to purify our desires and to consider what we may have allowed ourselves to neglect or compromise. Lent is the period not only to change our behavior but more important, to transform the condition of our hearts, our fundamental inner dispositions.

During Lent Benedict directs the monks to devote themselves "to prayer with tears, to lectio, to compunction of heart, and self-denial" (*Rule*, 49:4). All of these Lenten practices serve above all to transform the heart. There is an old monastic saying, *Si cor non orat, in vanum ligua laborat*—"If the heart does not pray, in vain does the tongue labor." This could be said of the Benedictine approach to liturgical prayer and lectio divina. In prayer the mouth and the heart must cooperate. "Compunction of heart" is both a penitential awareness of the reality of one's sinful condition and a deep desire to live fully in oneness with God. The source of the heart's compunction is the perceived difference between the heart's true self, which is made for God, and how false it has been.

For the sake of this transformation of the heart, Benedict emphasizes lectio divina during Lent. Through this attentive listening to the *sacra pagina* with "the ear of our heart" and prayerful reflection on these Scriptures in contemplative silence, we purify our desire for God and transform our lives from the inside to the outside. In this way, we may, as Benedict said, "with the joy of spiritual desire await holy Easter" (*Rule*, 49:7).

The Season of Growth and Transformation

The Scriptures of Lent have been chosen to provide us with images of transformation. They lead us from the desert to the flowing waters of baptism, from dark blindness to the dazzling light of resurrection, and from ashy decay and death to the new life of Easter.

The purpose of Lent is to nurture the seed of God's word, which lies lifeless and buried in the earth, so that it will grow, blossom, and produce fruit. We must make sure that the dryness of Lent's desert does not kill the sprouting seed. We must prevent Lent's painful thorns from choking off the growing plants. We must guarantee that our fasting does not diminish the nourishment that the word of God requires to flourish within us. We must, in other words, make sure we keep in mind the point of our Lenten disciplines—which is, according to St. Benedict, to increase the joy of spiritual longing with which we look forward to holy Easter.

The readings for Lent in the Lectionary of the Elect present these transforming images for the sake of those preparing for Easter's rebirth. On the crucial Third Sunday of Lent, Jesus promises the Samaritan woman the living waters of life. On the Fourth Sunday in the period of the Elect's enlightenment, Jesus heals the darkness of the man's blindness and gives him the light to see. On the Fifth Sunday, Jesus raises Lazarus from the dead and gives him new life. For the Elect and for all who continue longing for Christ, the Scriptures become truly a verbal icon of Christ. They fix our gaze on the person of Christ and lead us to contemplate the living Lord. By presenting Jesus himself as the Living Water, the Light of the World, and the Resurrection and the Life, these Scriptures prevent us from separating the words of the text from the living Word.

These forty days invite us to come into the desert with a deep desire for Christ. They invite us to join our lives with the Elect and the Penitents throughout the ages in their Lenten journeys. They urge us to support one another as we attend to whatever we have compromised or neglected up till now. They assure us that the dust and ashes of Lent's beginning form a fertile soil for the seeds of God's word to grow in our hearts and transform us. These forty days encourage us to nurture those seeds through lectio divina so that they may grow, leaf, blossom, and bear fruit in the joyful life of Easter.

Chapter Two

Lectio Divina for All God's People

L ectio divina is the church's most ancient way of studying Scripture. This ancient art is rooted in the Jewish tradition, and it has been nurtured through the desert spirituality of the early centuries, the patristic writers of the ancient church, and the monastic tradition through the ages. In today's worldwide revival of this age-old wisdom, Christians are learning how to experience Scripture in a deeper, more complete way by listening to and conversing with God through the inspired texts.

The only real purpose of lectio divina is to lead us to a personal encounter and dialogue with God. It is not a highly specialized method of prayer or a methodical system with required steps that must be rigidly followed.[1] The ancient spiritual masters always distrusted methods of prayer that were too severely defined. They knew that God's Spirit moves differently in each person and that God's inner work within the individual should not be impeded with unyielding rules. So there is no need to anxiously assess our spiritual practice as if we had to follow it "correctly" to achieve some particular target. There is no goal other than prayerfully reading Scripture in God's presence with a desire to deepen our heart-to-heart intimacy with him. In lectio divina we let go of our own agenda and gradually open

1 My previous work, *Conversing with God in Scripture: A Contemporary Approach to Lectio Divina*, explains how *The Monk's Ladder*, by the 12th century Carthusian monk Guigo II, unintentionally calcified the practice of lectio divina for subsequent centuries in a way that was far more rigidly and hierarchically defined than in the earlier centuries.

ourselves to what God wants us to experience through the *sacra pagina*, the inspired text.

The five components of lectio divina, which are outlined here, are best described as "movements," as distinguished from hierarchical steps or rungs on a ladder. This terminology allows for a certain amount of spontaneous freedom within the prayerful practice, as was characteristic of the practice in the church's early centuries.

Lectio: Reading the Text with a Listening Ear

We begin by setting aside the time and sanctifying the space for our reading. We might want to place a cross or icon in front of us, light a candle, or offer some gesture to highlight the moment. Placing the Bible or Lectionary text in our hands, we first call on the Holy Spirit to guide our minds and hearts in the presence of God's word.

We read the text slowly and attentively. We try to set aside any preconceived ideas about what the text is going to say. We read reverently and expectantly, knowing that God is going to speak to us in some new way, offering us some new wisdom and understanding through the inspired text.

Though lectio is often translated as "reading," the tradition suggests much more than ordinary reading. It is more like listening deeply. In lectio God is teaching us to listen to his voice within the words on the page. It often helps to return to the ancient practice of reading texts of Scripture aloud. In this way, we both see the text with our eyes and hear the words with our ears, encouraging a fuller comprehension and experience of the word.

Giving our whole attention to the words, we allow ourselves to enjoy the Scriptures. Savoring the words, images, metaphors, and characters, we grow to appreciate and love the text itself. Paying attention to its literary form, we realize that God's truth is expressed in a variety of ways through many types of literature in the Bible.

Biblical scholarship and commentary can help us understand more of the context of the passage by shedding light on what the authors meant to communicate in the text. The Jewish rabbinical tradition and the writings of church Fathers in the early centuries show us how artificial it is to make a distinction between the study of a text and prayerful reading. Grappling with the text, searching for fuller understanding, can be a prayerful and faith-filled process. The work of scholars can help us probe all the potential the text can offer us.

Finally, we must always ask how the writer's faith manifests itself in the text and what kind of faith response the writer wishes to elicit from us as readers. Emphasizing the faith dimension of a text helps us transcend the original circumstances in which it was written and allows us to see its lasting influence and universal validity.

Meditatio: Reflecting on the Meaning and Message of the Text

The eyes and ears and even the mind are not the final destination of God's word. We listen to the sacred text so that the words of Scripture might finally inhabit our hearts. When we have created space in our hearts for the word to dwell, the sacred texts can make their home in us, residing in the deepest part of our beings so that they become a part of us.

We can begin to open our hearts to God's word as we establish connections between the text of ancient times and our lives today. Either something in the text reminds us of something that has happened in our experience, or something that has happened reminds us of the text. In meditatio we ponder a text until it becomes like a mirror, reflecting some of our own experiences, challenges, thoughts, and questions.

When the patristic writers of the early church interpreted the Bible, they considered their work satisfactory only when they had found a meaning in the text that was relevant to the situation of Christians in their own day. Because God is the author of Scripture, he can speak to the present through the scriptural record of the past. As the word of God, the Bible has a richness that can be discovered in every age and in every culture. It has a particular message that can be received by every reader who listens to God's word in the context of his or her daily experiences.

A helpful way to meditate on a scriptural passage is to ask questions of the text. Some questions will help us make the connections: What aspects of the biblical world resemble our situation today? What aspects of our present condition does the text seem to address? What is the text's message for us right now? Other questions help us focus on more personal aspects of the text that we might want to reflect on in a deeper way: What emotions and memories does this text evoke in me? Where do I hear Christ speaking to me most personally in these verses? What grace is this text offering me? Often we will notice that rather than our questioning the Scriptures, they are questioning us. The text will challenge us to go beyond our current level of comfort and security: What attitudes or habits must I change in order to truly live these inspired words? Why am I so resistant to reflecting on this text more carefully? After reading a passage of the Bible, we shouldn't be surprised if it begins to read us.

The more we meditate on God's word, the more it seeps into our lives and saturates our thoughts and feelings. St. Ambrose, a fourth-century bishop and doctor of the church, described this assimilation: "When we drink from sacred Scripture, the life-sap of the eternal Word penetrates the veins of our soul and our inner faculties."[2] This is the purpose of meditatio. It allows the dynamic word of God to so penetrate our lives that it truly infuses our minds and hearts, and we begin to embody its truth and its love.

Oratio: Praying in Response to God's Word

Lectio divina is essentially a dialogue with God, a gentle oscillation between listening to God and responding to him in prayer. As we listen in a way that becomes increasingly more personal, as lectio moves into meditatio, we recognize that God is speaking to us and offering us a message that is unique to our own lives. Once we realize God's call to us, his personal challenge, or the insight he is trying to give us, we must answer in some way. This is the moment for prayer.

Our response to God in oratio is not just any form of prayer. In the context of lectio divina, oratio is rooted directly in prayerful reading and meditation on the scriptural text. In oratio the

2 Ambrose, *Commentaries on the Psalms* I, 33: *Patrologia Latina* 14, 984.

words, images, and sentiments of the biblical text combine with the ideas, feelings, memories, and desires arising within us. The words of Scripture, then, enter into our prayer language. The style and vocabulary of our personal prayers are enriched by the inspired words of our long biblical tradition. Our prayers no longer consist of repeated formulas, but they resonate with the faith, hope, and love that animated the people of the Bible in their journey with God.

The biblical words, then, that were at the center of our listening become also the heart of our response. Our prayer becomes a healthy combination of God's word and the words God moves us to say. The rich deposit God leaves within us after we have meditated on his word nourishes our prayer, so that it becomes a heartfelt and Spirit-led response to him. When our prayer does not arise from our listening and is separated from the biblical text, it can become excessively private, egotistical, or eccentric. But when our prayer remains close to the inspired page, we know that we are responding in a way that goes directly to the heart of God.

The tone of our prayer will depend on what we hear God saying to us in our lectio and meditatio. When the text reminds us of the goodness, truth, or beauty of God and his action in our lives, we pray in praise and thanksgiving. When it makes us aware of the wrong we have done or the good we have failed to do, we pray with repentance and seek forgiveness. When the text reminds us of our own needs or the needs of others, we pray in petition. In some cases, our prayer may even be a rebellion, a crying lament, or an angry tirade, as we see in the literature of Job, Jeremiah, and some of the psalms. The key to oratio is that our prayerful response to God flows directly from our listening.

The most essential element of oratio is desire. In fact, St. Augustine said, "The desire to pray is itself prayer."[3] Because we are made for God and only God satisfies our deepest longing, the greatest desire of the human heart is for God. Prayer happens at that moment when our desire for God meets God's desire for us. So when we pray, we are speaking with God, who knows us intimately, cares about us deeply, and accepts us unconditionally. When we discover an ability and desire to pray within our hearts, we know it is a gift of the Holy Spirit. In reality our desire for God is itself the presence of the Spirit working within us.

Contemplatio: Quietly Resting in God

The movement into contemplatio is a progression from conversation with God to communion with God. After listening to the Scriptures, reflecting on them, and responding to God in the words of our prayer, we then enter into silence. Resting in the divine presence, we simply accept and receive the transforming embrace of God who has led us to this moment.

Both oratio and contemplatio are prayer that arises from the heart. Oratio is word-filled prayer in response to God's word to us. Contemplatio is prayer with few if any words. It is the response to God that remains after words are no longer necessary or helpful. It is simply enjoying the experience of quietly being in God's presence. We no longer have a need to think or reason, listen or speak.

Of all the movements of lectio divina, contemplatio is the most difficult to describe because it is such a personal moment with God. But it is an essential part of the practice and should never be

---

3 Augustine, *Explanations of the Psalms*, 37, 14: *Patrologia Latina* 36, 404.

passed over. In fact, one could argue that contemplatio is the most essential element of lectio divina, even though it seems the most "useless" from a practical point of view.

Moving into contemplatio is always a matter of our receptivity to God's grace. Our task is to remove as many obstacles to God's Spirit as we can: our inner resistance, our fear of intimacy, our awareness of time, our desire to control the process, and our self-concern. We must remain lovingly attentive to God and experience the desire for interior silence. As we feel God drawing us into deeper awareness of his divine presence, we gradually abandon our intellectual activity and let ourselves be wooed into his embrace. The experience resembles that of lovers holding each other in wordless silence or of a sleeping child resting in the arms of its mother.

Though we might think that the movement of contemplatio is passive and uneventful, God's grace is truly at work in these moments, and the Holy Spirit is changing us from the inside without our awareness. In contemplatio our heart—the center of our being and the place where we are most truly ourselves—is humbly exposed to God. What happens within us during those moments is something beyond our control. Contemplatio slowly works at transforming our hearts, offering us a taste of the divine life we are destined to share completely. Though there is often no sign of God at work in the silence, his invisible and unknowable presence is working to transform us at the deepest level.

Operatio: Faithful Witness in Daily Life

Through lectio divina, God's word shapes us and impacts our lives. After reading, reflecting, and praying over the word, we should be changed in some specific and concrete way. The changes we experience can be as simple as an adjusted attitude toward our work and a kindness to someone in need, or they can be as demanding as an urgency to change our career or reconcile with someone with whom we've been estranged. Operatio is this lived response to the inspired word.

Through lectio divina we evangelize ourselves, building bridges between the text and daily life. Every biblical text has a call or challenge to those who listen and respond to its sacred words. Operatio is the fruit we bear from nurturing the word of God through our listening, reflecting, and praying. We gradually realize that the fruit of lectio divina is the fruit of the Spirit: "love, joy, peace, patience, kindness, generosity, faithfulness, gentleness, and self-control" (Galatians 5:22-23). When we begin to notice this fruit in the way we live each day, we will know that the word of God is having its effect within us. In operatio we become witnesses to God's kingdom and living members of Christ's body in the world.

Contemplatio and operatio grow together in the heart of one who prayerfully reads Scripture. The word of God draws us inward to that deep place inside ourselves where we find God; it also impels us outward to those places in need of the light of the divine word. Apart from operatio, contemplatio becomes passive introspection. Apart from contemplatio, operatio becomes superficial pragmatism.

Contemplatio cultivates compassion within us. It enables us to see the deepest meaning and significance of issues, problems, and events. Only when we have attained the understanding and compassion that contemplatio nurtures can our action in the world be a genuine work of God's Spirit. Throughout history many of

Christianity's most ardent activists have also been the most fervent contemplatives. Lectio divina helps us to be contemplative activists and active contemplatives.

Lectio divina is not so much a matter of interpreting a written text as of seeking Christ and learning to be his disciple. He is the living Word to whom all the other words of Scripture bear witness. Through listening, reflecting, and praying on Scripture, our hearts and minds are formed in the way of Christ, as we deepen our relationship with him. As we develop this personal bond with Christ, our actions become an imitation of Christ and vehicles of his presence to others.

As our discipleship deepens through lectio divina, we seek to be totally identified with Christ. We desire to live "in Christ," and we experience Christ working within us, with our lives animated by his Spirit. Rather than wanting to imitate Christ, we begin to experience Christ working through us, and our actions become more his work than our own. In contemplatio, Christ prays within us, and in operatio, Christ becomes the doer of our actions. In this mystical bond with Christ, we see the true depth of discipleship that lectio divina can create within us.

Chapter Three

Lectio Divina for Lent: Year A

First Sunday of Lent

LECTIO

Close off the distractions of the day and enter a still moment for your time with the inspired word. Inhale and exhale slowly, becoming aware of your breathing as you recognize each breath as a gift from God. Breathe in, being filled with the presence of God's Spirit. Breathe out, letting go of all that could distract you from this sacred time.

Begin reading when you feel ready to hear God's voice. Read this familiar text as if for the first time, trying to let go of your own presumptions so that you can listen to God speaking to you anew.

GENESIS 2:7-9; 3:1-7

The LORD God formed man out of the clay of the ground and blew into his nostrils the breath of life, and so man became a living being.

Then the LORD God planted a garden in Eden, in the east, and placed there the man whom he had formed. Out of the ground the LORD God made various trees grow that were delightful to look at and good for food, with the tree of life in the middle of the garden and the tree of the knowledge of good and evil.

Now the serpent was the most cunning of all the animals that the LORD God had made. The serpent asked the woman, "Did God really tell you not to eat from any of the trees in the garden?" The woman answered the serpent: "We may eat of the fruit of the trees in the garden; it is only about the fruit of the tree in the middle of the garden that God said, 'You shall not eat it or even touch it, lest you die.'" But the serpent said to the woman: "You certainly will not die! No, God knows well that the moment you eat of it your eyes will be opened and you will be like gods who know what is good and what is evil." The woman saw that the tree was good for food, pleasing to the eyes, and desirable for gaining wisdom. So she took some of its fruit and ate it; and she also gave some to her husband, who was with her, and he ate it. Then the eyes of both of them were opened, and they realized that they were naked; so they sewed fig leaves together and made loincloths for themselves.

This colorful account of creation and sin is so rich in images and symbolism that commentators have spent volumes exploring its allusions and implications. God forms the human (*'adam* in Hebrew) from the ground (*'adama* in Hebrew). God gives life to his clay creature by breathing in the divine breath. Lovingly shaped by God and infused with his very spirit, the human creature is a masterpiece of our creating God. The Creator places his newly fashioned human in a garden full of beautiful and nourishing trees. This bountiful God not only offers gifts in abundance but also permeates the garden with his presence and continually offers care and companionship.

After pausing to let the words and images sink in, begin reading the gospel when you are ready. You will move from the lush garden to the dry desert. Read this familiar account, too, as if for the first time. Listen with expectation, confident that God will teach you something new through the words of the Gospel according to Matthew.

MATTHEW 4:1-11

At that time Jesus was led by the Spirit into the desert to be tempted by the devil. He fasted for forty days and forty nights, and afterwards he was hungry. The tempter approached and said to him, "If you are the Son of God, command that these stones become loaves of bread." He said in reply, "It is written:

> One does not live on bread alone,
>> but on every word that comes forth
>> from the mouth of God."

Then the devil took him to the holy city, and made him stand on the parapet of the temple, and said to him, "If you are the Son of God, throw yourself down. For it is written:

> He will command his angels concerning you
>> and with their hands they will support you,
>> lest you dash your foot against a stone."

Jesus answered him, "Again it is written, *You shall not put the Lord, your God, to the test.*" Then the devil took him up to a very high mountain, and showed him all the kingdoms of the world in their magnificence, and he said to him, "All these I shall give to you, if you will prostrate yourself and worship me." At this, Jesus said to him, "Get away, Satan! It is written:

> *The Lord, your God, shall you worship*
> *and him alone shall you serve."*

Then the devil left him and, behold, angels came and ministered to him.

The juxtaposition of the verdant garden and the barren desert highlights the contrast in these two scenes as the human couple and Jesus himself are put to the test. In each narrative, the subjects are tested in their fidelity to their identity and their obedience to God's will. The tempter in the garden and in the desert distorts the word of God and uses it to his own advantage. He confronts his prey with timeless temptations—to deny who they are, to overreach and take what is not theirs, to want to be "like God," to deny that God can ask them to trust their greatest good to him.

In the story of the garden, we sometimes fail to realize that God's permission is far wider than his prohibition. God permits the couple almost total freedom and access to the riches of the garden, and he provides them abundant life, meaningful purpose, and harmonious relationships. God prohibits the fruit of only one tree, because eating from that tree leads to death. It is their condition of restraint so that they may continue to enjoy the fullness of life.

But when the cunning serpent enters the garden, he distorts God's permission and prohibition concerning the fruit of the trees.

With enticing seduction, the serpent goes on to deny that death would be the inevitable consequence for rejecting the limitations God has placed on them. The tempter suggests instead that the woman and man would be like God, possessing great knowledge and able to determine for themselves what is good and what is evil. The Lord of the garden, who has bestowed such wondrous gifts and abundant freedom, is presented by the serpent as one who wants to confine rather than provide. The safe boundaries God has established for the couple's well-being in the garden now seem to them like a restriction upon their freedom and autonomy.

After considering the serpent's distorted line of reasoning and her newly acquired desire to taste the tree's fruit, the woman takes some of its fruit and eats it. Then she gives some to her husband, who is with her, and he eats it. There is no sense here that the woman enticed the man to disobedience. They were both present during the testing, and each of them ate freely. They act in total accord and sin as a pair. By refusing to trust God and his loving will for them, their choice brings shame and fear, mistrust of God and one another, and evasion of responsibility.

This ancient story offers profound insight into the human predicament. Through representational figures, symbolic language, and Hebrew wordplays, the narrator speaks to and about all women and men. The desires and responses of the man and the woman, and consequently their dilemma, characterize the experience of all humankind. The transgression depicted is not simply the first sin, it is all human sin; it is my sin. We who listen to this ancient story know that our sin, too, has cosmic dimensions, that our transgressions influence the relationship of humankind with God, that our failure to heed the boundaries that God has established affects the trustful relationship he wishes to share with his people.

The gospel scene in the desert presents Jesus being tested in his fidelity to his identity and in his obedience to his Father. While the tempter distorts and misuses the Scriptures, Jesus is shown to be the one who listens to God's word and fully embodies the Scriptures in his own life. Jesus does not overreach his messianic role, misuse his power, or allow his liberty to become license. His power and freedom do not become self-serving, but are put in service of his divine mission.

As the new Adam, Jesus Christ supplants the sin of humankind and personifies the life of grace. What humanity did through disobedience, Christ has undone through his obedience. Where humanity failed, Christ succeeded. Where death reigned through sin, so much more will life reign through the love of Christ that led to the cross.

MEDITATIO

The challenge of meditatio is to continue reflecting on the scriptural narratives until they become a mirror in which we see our own reflection. Recognize within the text your own temptations, sins, challenges, and failures.

- The dust of the ground (our material reality) and the breath/spirit of God (our spiritual reality) are both good, both gifts of God and important elements of our human existence. Both must be kept in balance if we are to live in harmony with God, ourselves, other people, and with the rest of creation. What happens to that harmony if we smother the spirit? What happens if we deny the dust?

- How is Lent the right time to focus on the balance between our dust and our spirit? How can the disciplines of Lent help you maintain harmony with God, within yourself, with other people, and with the rest of creation?

- Through human choice, God's purpose for man and woman, with its wide permission and necessary prohibition, is disturbed and distorted. What new understandings have you gained by reading these passages afresh, "as if for the first time"?

- Humanity's perennial temptation is to usurp the power of the Creator and to use that power for self-serving purposes. Reflect on humanity's drive for control of nature and other people, and consider the massive horrors that have resulted over the last century from the human quest for unlimited power. How can the issues of power and dominance distort God's purposes for your life?

- Jesus resisted the primal temptation toward misuse of power while emptying himself to experience true power. His temptations in the desert strengthened him for his final conquest of sin on the cross. How is my human effort less a conquest of sin and more a surrender to Christ?

ORATIO

⋏

Cry out to God in the midst of your trial and testing, knowing that he has conquered sin in his Son Jesus and gives you the strength to overcome the creaturely tendency to rebel, revolt, and diminish your humanity.

Begin with this prayer and continue to pray as your heart directs you:

I cry out to you, Creator God, to help me know my true identity, created in your image and destined for life in its fullness. Help me to live as a creature of dust and spirit, humbly aware of my frailty and attentive to my eternal dignity.

CONTEMPLATIO

⋏

In your imagination, place yourself either in the garden or the desert. Know that God is with you there with his encouraging and supportive presence. Place yourself completely in God's care, trusting in his unlimited grace. Remain in this place for a period of prolonged silence.

OPERATIO

⋏

Consider how God is molding and shaping you through this experience of lectio divina. How is your mind or heart different after having prayerfully reflected on these Lenten narratives? What does God want from you during this week of Lent?

Second Sunday of Lent

LECTIO

Place a cross or icon in front of you, light a candle, or find another visible symbol to help sanctify and purify the space you have chosen to hear God's word. Call upon the same Holy Spirit who inspired the sacred writers to fill your heart and kindle in you the fire of divine love.

Read aloud, vocalizing the words of the text so that you not only read with your eyes but hear with your ears. Listen to God's word with the ears of your heart.

GENESIS 12:1-4A

The LORD said to Abram: "Go forth from the land of your kinsfolk and from your father's house to a land that I will show you.

"I will make of you a great nation,
and I will bless you;
I will make your name great,
so that you will be a blessing.
I will bless those who bless you
and curse those who curse you.
All the communities of the earth
shall find blessing in you."
Abram went as the LORD directed him.

Abraham's journey is the primordial faith narrative for all believers. God called Abram (later named Abraham) to "Go forth" (Genesis 12:1), and without knowing where he was going, "Abraham went" (12:4). God's call demanded that he leave the region of Mesopotamia, his ethnic group, and his extended family, which were the basis of his security, trade, and identity. Abram's act of obedience began a life that would make him the father of faith, an example for all who would follow in his lineage of what it means to believe. He not only accepted with his mind whatever God revealed, but he also said yes with his life to whatever God wanted.

At the center of Abram's call are the wondrous promises of God. These promises are the key to the entire Bible and will be fulfilled throughout the history of salvation. The initial set of promises expresses God's commitment to Abram: first, to make of him a great nation; second, to bless him with abundant flocks and numerous offspring, good health, and long life; and third, to make his name great so that he will be esteemed with a noble reputation. The second set of promises shows how God will affect other nations through Abram with blessings and curses. What is most amazing is that God proclaims the highest goal of Abram's calling: "All the communities of the earth shall find blessing in you" (Genesis 12:3). Through Abraham and his descendants, God will bestow universal blessings to all the people of the world.

After quietly considering the scene of Abraham's call and its universal implications, begin reading the gospel. You will move from the river valley of Abraham's homeland to a high mountain in the land God promised. Read this gospel account with new eyes, listening to God's word and imagining this wondrous scene.

MATTHEW 17:1-9

Jesus took Peter, James, and John his brother, and led them up a high mountain by themselves. And he was transfigured before them; his face shone like the sun and his clothes became white as light. And behold, Moses and Elijah appeared to them, conversing with him. Then Peter said to Jesus in reply, "Lord, it is good that we are here. If you wish, I will make three tents here, one for you, one for Moses, and one for Elijah." While he was still speaking, behold, a bright cloud cast a shadow over them, then from the cloud came a voice that said, "This is my beloved Son, with whom I am well pleased; listen to him." When the disciples heard this, they fell prostrate and were very much afraid. But Jesus came and touched them, saying, "Rise, and do not be afraid." And when the disciples raised their eyes, they saw no one else but Jesus alone.

As they were coming down from the mountain, Jesus charged them, "Do not tell the vision to anyone until the Son of Man has been raised from the dead."

Along with the beginnings of faith with Abraham, the lives of Moses and Elijah, representing the Torah and the prophets, embody the whole of God's ancient revelation to Israel. As they appear with the transfigured Jesus on the mountaintop, we realize that this vision expresses the climactic fulfillment of God's saving mission to bring blessings to all the people of the world.

The transfiguration occurs in the gospel as Jesus begins his journey to Jerusalem, the journey of faith that will lead to the cross. Though Abraham did not know where his journey would direct him, Jesus knows his journey's goal and the sacrifice it entails. Yet as God reinforced Abraham's call with wonderful promises, he heartens the way of Jesus and his disciples with this vision of transfigured glory.

The transformed face and garments of Jesus express the glory of God and Jesus' holy identity. Moses and Elijah were spiritual ancestors who both went to the mountain, to Mount Sinai, to experience the glory of God, which would sustain them on their obedient journey of faith and suffering for the people of God (Exodus 19; 1 Kings 19). Jesus follows in their way and brings their saving path to its glorious culmination.

As Abraham, Moses, and Elijah preceded Jesus and prepared his way, Peter, James, and John travel with Jesus to Jerusalem and will continue his way into the early church. Not knowing where the journey will lead, their path with Jesus will form models of Christian discipleship for future generations. Through the failures and successes of their example, their struggles to believe and accept and follow, countless others will continue in the way of Jesus to bring blessings to all the people of the world.

The biblical narratives of Abraham, Moses, and Elijah, together with the life of Jesus and his disciples, teach us that the Christian life is a journey in faith. Peter's instincts were right to suggest erecting tents on the spot. Those tents were the temporary, makeshift shelters erected during the Jewish Feast of Sukkoth to remember Israel's forty-year journey through the desert. Peter's recognition of the journey reminds us that we are indeed people of the Way, on the path of discipleship.

It is the divine voice from the cloud that points to the way of full discipleship. Acknowledging Jesus as his beloved Son, God says, "Listen to him" (Matthew 17:5). Listening to Jesus is the way to follow in his footsteps: listening to the word of God that transfigures sinners into forgiven and redeemed people, that transfigures sick and disabled bodies into healed and whole beings, that transfigures bread and wine into his body and blood, that transfigures suffering and death into resurrected life.

MEDITATIO

Spend some time reflecting on the narratives you have read, allowing them to interact with your own world of memories, questions, ideas, and concerns, until you are aware of the personal messages the texts offer to you.

- Abraham left a legacy that extended further than anyone could imagine because he had the vision to see beyond his own lifetime and the wisdom to understand the importance of making sacrifices for future generations. What kind of legacy would you like to leave for the future?

- Abraham not only accepted with his mind whatever God revealed but he said yes with his life to whatever God wanted. How ready are you to listen and say yes? What does Abraham teach you about the journey of faith?

- Why did Jesus show his transfigured glory to his disciples at the beginning of their journey to Jerusalem? What keeps you engaged and motivated along the path of discipleship?

- In the biblical languages, "to listen" means both to hear and to obey. God tells the disciples to listen to Jesus as he teaches them the way of discipleship on the journey toward Jerusalem. As you reflect on God's command "to listen" to Jesus, what are you being challenged to believe or to do?

- These texts join the most important personages of the Old Testament with the most significant individuals of the New Testament. What does the whole narrative represented by these characters teach you about believing God, accepting his will, and following his way?

ORATIO

After listening and reflecting on the word of God, respond to that word with heartfelt and embodied prayer.

Let this prayer be an incentive to continue with your own:

God of our ancestors, you call people in every age to walk in faith and bring blessings to your people. Teach me to listen to your Son, so that I may obey and follow in the way you desire for my life. Help me make a difference in the lives of others and leave a legacy of faith to the next generation.

Continue to pray in whatever words your heart directs.

CONTEMPLATIO

Imaginatively place yourself at the mountaintop with Christ. Feel his transfigured presence enlightening your mind and enflaming your heart. Let the voice of God saying "Listen to him" resonate within you. Spend some time in the quiet majesty of this moment.

OPERATIO

As you prayerfully reflect on Scripture, lectio divina gradually but ultimately transfigures you into a greater expression of the mystery of Christ. In what way do you sense yourself being transformed into the presence of Christ for others this Lent? How can you express your transformed life through Christlike actions this week?

Third Sunday of Lent

LECTIO

Place a bowl of water, a fountain, or some other symbol of refreshment before you to calm your mind as you read these texts. Separate this time and space from the rest of your day so that you may be ready to truly hear the words of these inspired texts.

Highlight, underline, circle, and mark up the text as a way to focus on your reading. This will help you to pay attention in a new way as you read.

EXODUS 17:3-7

In those days, in their thirst for water, the people grumbled against Moses, saying, "Why did you ever make us leave Egypt? Was it just to have us die here of thirst with our children and our livestock?" So Moses cried out to the LORD, "What shall I do with this people? A little more and they will stone me!" The LORD answered Moses, "Go over there in front of the people, along with some of the elders of Israel, holding in your hand, as you go, the staff with which you struck the river. I will be standing there in front of you on the rock in Horeb. Strike the rock, and the water will flow from it for the people to drink." This Moses did, in the presence of the elders of Israel. The place was called Massah and Meribah, because the Israelites quarreled there and tested the LORD, saying, "Is the LORD in our midst or not?"

In the arid lands in which most of the events in the Bible occur, people are acutely aware of the perils of being without water. Dying of thirst is always a frightening possibility. The writers recognize that God is the one who ultimately quenches thirst. Usually God brings water through natural processes such as rain and springs, but sometimes that provision is given through extraordinary means as when he brings water from the rock along Israel's journey through the desert.

The people of Israel demonstrate a lack of trust in God's providential care, and they fear death by dehydration in the wilderness. Regretting their departure from Egypt where water was plentiful, they ask, "Is the Lord in our midst of not?" (Exodus 17:7). Such doubt is amazing considering God's deliverance of Israel from slavery, God's rescue at the sea, and God's direction and sustenance in the desert. As God said through the psalmist, "They tested me though they had seen my works" (Psalm 95:9).

God works through Moses and his staff to provide water for the people to drink. In this passage, as well as the many other passages about thirst and water in the Bible, the flowing water expresses God's satisfaction of his people's deepest needs, both physical and spiritual. Here Moses strikes the rock, and life-giving water flows from what is hard and dry. During Lent God calls us to strike the rock of our hard hearts with the rods of fasting, prayer, and almsgiving. When we open our spiritual core to God, he will make flow within us the life-giving spring of grace.

Allow a few moments of quiet to let the inspired word soak into your thirsting heart. When you are ready, listen carefully to the words of John's Gospel.

JOHN 4:5-15, 19B-26, 39A, 40-42

Jesus came to a town of Samaria called Sychar, near the plot of land that Jacob had given to his son Joseph. Jacob's well was there. Jesus, tired from his journey, sat down there at the well. It was about noon.

A woman of Samaria came to draw water. Jesus said to her, "Give me a drink." His disciples had gone into the town to buy food. The Samaritan woman said to him, "How can you, a Jew, ask me, a Samaritan woman, for a drink?" —For Jews use nothing in common with Samaritans.— Jesus answered and said to her, "If you knew the gift of God and who is saying to you, 'Give me a drink,' you would have asked him and he would have given you living water." The woman said to him, "Sir, you do not even have a bucket and the cistern is deep; where then can you get this living water? Are you greater than our father Jacob, who gave us this cistern and drank from it himself with his children and his flocks?" Jesus answered and said to her, "Everyone who drinks this water will be thirsty again; but whoever drinks the water I shall give will never thirst; the water I shall give will become in him a spring of water welling up to eternal life." The woman said to him, "Sir, give me this water, so that I may not be thirsty or have to keep coming here to draw water.

"I can see that you are a prophet. Our ancestors worshiped on this mountain; but you people say that the place to worship is in Jerusalem." Jesus said to her, "Believe me, woman, the hour is coming when you will worship the Father neither on this mountain nor in Jerusalem. You people worship what you do not understand; we worship what we understand, because salvation is from the Jews. But the hour is coming, and is now here, when true worshipers will worship the Father in Spirit and truth; and indeed the Father seeks such people to worship him. God is Spirit, and those who worship him must worship in Spirit and truth." The woman said to him, "I know that the Messiah is coming, the one called the Christ; when he comes, he will tell us everything." Jesus said to her, "I am he, the one speaking with you."

Many of the Samaritans of that town began to believe in him because of the word of the woman. When the Samaritans came to him, they invited him to stay with them; and he stayed there two days. Many more began to believe in him because of his word, and they said to the woman, "We no longer believe because of your word; for we have heard for ourselves, and we know that this is truly the savior of the world."

Throughout the Bible the well is a place of commitment and betrothal. It was at a well that Jacob met Rachel (Genesis 29:10) and where Moses met his future wife, Zipporah (Exodus 2:15-21). Here Jesus encounters the Samaritan woman, breaking gender, ethnic, and religious boundaries, in order to "woo" this woman to committed faith. He begins on the level of human needs, admitting his own weariness and thirst from his journey, and asks the woman for a drink of water from the well. Building on the foundation of human need, Jesus moves to the deeper truth.

"Living water" has a double meaning: it is fresh, flowing water and water that gives life. This water has a replenishing, renewing source, whereas motionless water must be continually replaced lest it grow stagnant. Jesus tells the woman that the water he gives continually springs up from the limitless generosity of God. This living water has an inner source that provides continual replenishment so that the bearer will never thirst again.

God is the provider of this life-giving water. It is God's living word, empowered by his sanctifying Spirit. It echoes Jesus' offer to Nicodemus of new birth from water and the Holy Spirit (John 3). When this water springs up from within our hearts, we are able to worship God "in Spirit and truth" (4:23), and we become bearers of that life to others. The woman urgently went to tell the people of Samaria about the man who lowered a bucket deep into her heart and drew up living water from within her.

During the Third, Fourth, and Fifth Sundays of Lent, we hear three narratives from John's Gospel, which were chosen for Lent from its earliest days. Their rich symbolism of water, light, and life provides an ideal catechesis for those preparing for baptism. They expound upon the journey of coming to faith, teaching the seeker that life need not end ultimately in dust and ashes. They help the Elect understand Christ, God's living Word, and what it means to live in him.

The Samaritan woman receives from Jesus the water of eternal life, which quenches her deepest thirsts. From the water's deep source within her, she draws life and gives testimony to Jesus the Messiah. For those preparing to enter the water of Easter baptism, she is a model for their journey of faith. For those of us who are already baptized, she teaches us to thirst for the water that truly quenches, to allow Jesus to evoke from within us the faith and testimony that proclaim that he is "truly the Savior of the world" (John 4:42).

MEDITATIO

Allow the revitalizing water of God's word to spring up and flow within you. Let that word refresh you and spill over you, soaking you with abundant life in God's Spirit.

- When Moses struck the rock with his rod, life-giving water flowed for all the people to drink. In what ways are my Lenten disciplines striking my rocky heart to open the way for the springs of God's grace?

- Jesus broke the barriers that separated Jews from Samaritans and took the initiative in asking the woman for a drink. In what ways does life in Christ encourage you to transcend boundaries that separate people by nationality, ethnicity, gender, and other distinctions?

- Thirst for water is one of the most popular biblical metaphors for the human longing for God. Isaiah proclaimed, "All you who are thirsty, come to the water!" (55:1). When is my yearning for God dehydrated? Thirsty? Quenched? Saturated?

- This gospel is chosen for Lent because it teaches the Elect how to prepare for baptism, and it teaches the baptized how to be renewed in Christ. What do you think are the most important aspects of life in Christ that are highlighted by this gospel narrative?

• After coming to faith in Jesus, the woman went to the Samaritans in her town to tell them of her experience. Many of the Samaritans there began to believe in Jesus because of her testimony. Why and how does conversion lead to evangelization?

ORATIO

God thirsts for us, so we listen. We thirst for God, so we pray. Lectio divina is the encounter of God's thirst with ours. Let these words be your prayer starter:

Merciful God, we were created with hearts thirsting for you. Draw forth the springs of your Holy Spirit from within me so that I can experience the abundance of your life.

Continue to pray whatever words well up from the depths of your heart.

CONTEMPLATIO

Pause from your long Lenten journey and recognize your thirst for God. Contemplate the living springs of God's word that he wants to offer your thirsting heart. Receive the refreshment God is presenting to you.

OPERATIO

Consider the transforming effects of your lectio divina as you journey through Lent. In what way is God preparing you for the liturgies of the sacred Triduum and Easter? What additional spiritual practice could you do this week to open yourself more fully to God's ongoing renewal of your life?

Fourth Sunday of Lent

LECTIO

Light a candle or place some other visible symbol before you to help you focus on God's living word. Call upon the Holy Spirit to enlighten your eyes and your heart as you read the sacred text.

Begin reading when you are prepared to encounter God through the words of these inspired Scriptures.

1 SAMUEL 16:1B, 6-7, 10-13A

The LORD said to Samuel: "Fill your horn with oil, and be on your way. I am sending you to Jesse of Bethlehem, for I have chosen my king from among his sons."

As Jesse and his sons came to the sacrifice, Samuel looked at Eliab and thought, "Surely the LORD's anointed is here before him." But the LORD said to Samuel: "Do not judge from his appearance or from his lofty stature, because I have rejected him. Not as man sees does God see, because man sees the appearance but the LORD looks into the heart." In the same way Jesse presented seven sons before Samuel, but Samuel said to Jesse, "The LORD has not chosen any one of these." Then Samuel asked Jesse, "Are these all the sons you have?" Jesse replied, "There is still the youngest, who is tending the sheep." Samuel said to Jesse, "Send for him; we will not begin the sacrificial banquet until he arrives here." Jesse sent and had the young man brought to them. He was ruddy, a youth handsome to behold and making a splendid appearance. The LORD said, "There—anoint him, for this is the one!" Then Samuel, with the horn of oil in hand, anointed David in the presence of his brothers; and from that day on, the spirit of the LORD rushed upon David.

This first appearance of David in the Bible marks the beginning of a new era in God's history of salvation. Samuel is divinely charged to anoint Israel's king. This is no historical accident or political ploy; God has instructed Samuel to fill his horn with oil and set out for the household of Jesse in Bethlehem, for God has already made his selection: "I have chosen my king from among his sons" (1 Samuel 16:1).

When Jesse and his sons come to the sacrifice, Samuel seeks to know which one of the seven is God's appointed. Seeing Jesse's oldest son, Eliab, Samuel is impressed by his height and physical appearance. When Samuel assumes this must be the one God has chosen, God warns him that mortals see only the exterior appearance, "but the LORD looks into the heart" (1 Samuel 16:7). Only after Jesse's seven sons have all passed before Samuel and he realizes that God has not chosen any of them does Jesse admit there is another—his youngest son, who is keeping the sheep. Putting the sacrificial banquet on hold, Samuel insists that this one be brought before him before the feast can begin.

The household of Jesse and the elders of Bethlehem all wait in anticipation. As Israel has waited through the centuries, now all the characters and readers of the drama await the arrival of David. While the crowd is watching for David, the young shepherd is watching his flock—leading his sheep to pasture, strengthening the weak, binding the broken, and seeking out the lost. The young, insignificant, lowly, and marginalized one is about to enter history and change everything.

When the youthful shepherd arrives on the scene, God says, "This is the one" (1 Samuel 16:12). Samuel immediately anoints David by pouring the oil over his head, and in that moment, "the spirit of the LORD" (16:3), God's wind and breath, rushes upon him, from that day forward. God has designated his king, and a new era has begun. The shepherd of the flock in Bethlehem will rule as "shepherd" of all God's people in Jerusalem.

JOHN 9:1, 6-9, 13-17, 34-38

As Jesus passed by he saw a man blind from birth. Jesus spat on the ground and made clay with the saliva, and smeared the clay on his eyes, and said to him, "Go wash in the Pool of Siloam"—which means Sent—. So he went and washed, and came back able to see.

His neighbors and those who had seen him earlier as a beggar said, "Isn't this the one who used to sit and beg?" Some said, "It is," but others said, "No, he just looks like him." He said, "I am."

They brought the one who was once blind to the Pharisees. Now Jesus had made clay and opened his eyes on a sabbath. So then the Pharisees also asked him how he was able to see. He said to them, "He put clay on my eyes, and I washed, and now I can see." So some of the Pharisees said, "This man is not from God, because he does not keep the sabbath." But others said, "How can a sinful man do such signs?" And there was a division among them. So they said to the blind man again, "What do you have to say about him, since he opened your eyes?" He said, "He is a prophet."

They answered and said to him, "You were born totally in sin, and are you trying to teach us?" Then they threw him out.

When Jesus heard that they had thrown him out, he found him and said, "Do you believe in the Son of Man?" He answered and said, "Who is he, sir, that I may believe in him?" Jesus said to him, "You have seen him, the one speaking with you is he." He said, "I do believe, Lord," and he worshiped him.

Creation is always a work in progress. Since the beginning of creation to the present, the work of God has been bringing light out of darkness. As the light of the world, Jesus has been sent to do just that. In order to bring sight to the man born blind, Jesus takes up the original substance from which God created the man and fashions the clay on the blind man's eyes. He is not creating the man again, but completing his creation. Jesus ultimately intends to activate the blind man's undeveloped spiritual sight in order to bring his creation to its completion.

The blind man must also do his part. He must obey Jesus and go to the Pool of Siloam to wash his eyes. He will then be able to see, and thereby become a witness, not only to his physical cure, but to the opening of the eyes of his heart to the truth of Jesus.

After the blind man washes his eyes in the pool and is able to see, the story moves from the visible sign to its foundational meaning. When challenged by the Pharisees, the man who was formerly blind is astonished by his cure, but he does not understand it. He simply tells them what he had experienced: "He put clay on my eyes, and I washed, and now I can see" (John 9:15). But while the Pharisees stumble in the darkness, they are unsuspectingly helping the man move toward the light as he confesses that Jesus must be a prophet.

Jesus is determined to finish what he started, so he seeks out the man again. When the man who can now see states his desire to believe, Jesus replies, "You have seen him" (John 9:37), a word-play on sight, suggesting that the real vision given to the man is that of faith. As Jesus, the Light of the world, shines into the man's last darkness, he is brought to full illumination. As he sees clearly, faith flows from him in words—"I do believe, Lord"—and in deeds—"he worshiped him" (9:38). Through the narrative, the man moves from spiritual blindness, to acknowledging Jesus to be a prophet, to believing in him as Son of Man, to finally worshiping him as Lord. God's creation of the blind man is now complete.

The deepest truth of this gospel narrative is that we are all born blind. The initiative of Jesus, his amazing grace, offers us sight. During our journey of Lent, the motif of washing in the pool leading to sight anticipates baptism at Easter. As we support the Elect through this period of purification and enlightenment, we seek to imitate the journey of the man in the gospel as we progress toward inner illumination and greater insight about Jesus. Lent is a time to become aware of our own blindness, to acknowledge the ways we fail to live our baptismal faith, and to seek a clearer, more enlightened vision.

MEDITATIO

⋏

Let these Scriptures touch your heart by reflecting on them in light of your own experiences of blindness and your struggles to see clearly.

- God said to Samuel, "Not as man sees does God see, because man sees the appearance but the LORD looks into the heart" (1 Samuel 16:7). What does God see in you that is not obvious to the world? In what way is God's choice of David a prototype of God's choice of you?

- Like the gospel texts from the previous and the subsequent Sundays, this proclamation from the Gospel of John is one of the oldest texts for Lent because of its teaching about the journey of coming to faith. In what ways does this text shed light on your own journey of coming to faith and what it means to live in Christ?

- Christ calls his church to be a light for the world, to illumine the earth with his truth and life. Scrutinize your life and recognize some of those dark places where Christ has not penetrated. What can you do to help bring light to the dark areas of Christ's church?

- Spiritual blindness is simply the raw, unfinished part of creation that God uses to bring forth light. But the light of Christ requires a decision on the part of each person, either to rise into the light or to sink into the darkness. What are some of your struggles in opening your life more fully to the Light of the world?

- God desires to complete our creation in Christ. In what ways do you need to be molded and formed by the Creator's hand in order to deepen your faith and be able to see yourself more completely as God's masterpiece?

ORATIO

It is God's grace at work within us that gives us a desire to pray. Touch that deep desire within you and respond to God in prayer. Begin with these words:

Creator God, you have sculpted our lives from clay and fashioned our eyes to see. Continue your creative work within me, reshaping my flaws and giving me clearer vision. Help me realize the purpose you have given my life in Christ and illumine my path for the journey ahead.

Continue to expose your heart to God as you pray in whatever way you choose.

CONTEMPLATIO

God said to Samuel, "Man sees the appearance but the LORD looks into the heart" (1 Samuel 16:7). When the words of prayer are no longer necessary or helpful, move into a wordless silence in the divine presence. Open your heart to God and trust that God is working deep within you to fashion you into his masterpiece.

OPERATIO

The crowd in the gospel asked the man, "What do you have to say about him, since he opened your eyes?" (John 9:17). Carry this question with you this week and ask yourself how you are called to be a witness to Jesus.

Fifth Sunday of Lent

LECTIO

As you prepare for your attentive listening to God's word, breathe in, being filled with the presence of God's Spirit. Breathe out, letting go of all that could distract you from this sacred time.

Read these texts aloud, seeking to hear God's word within them, without any presumptions. Listen to them in a new way, guided by God's renewing Spirit.

EZEKIEL 37:12-14

Thus says the Lord GOD: O my people, I will open your graves and have you rise from them, and bring you back to the land of Israel. Then you shall know that I am the LORD, when I open your graves and have you rise from them, O my people! I will put my spirit in you that you may live, and I will settle you upon your land; thus you shall know that I am the LORD. I have promised, and I will do it, says the LORD.

The prophet Ezekiel spoke to the people of Israel during the darkest time of their history. The Babylonians had destroyed Jerusalem, burned down the Temple, and sent many Israelites into exile. Any reason for hope seemed gone, and God's people felt as good as dead.

Ezekiel preached a positive message to a people who experienced their lives as doomed. In the verses that precede this text, he offers the vision of the valley of dry bones. At God's command, the scattered bones form into skeletons and take on sinew and flesh, and God's life-giving breath returns them to life. The dry bones are the people of Israel in exile: broken in spirit, bereft of hope, cut off from their source of life.

The prophet then offers this oracle of hope. God will raise the Israelites from their graves of despair and give them life again as a people. He will plant them firmly once more in the land he has ordained for them. It is God's spirit who animates them, gathers them again as a people, and gives them the will to embrace their future.

We've all been in the valley of the dry bones, feeling as though we are among the dead walking in the midst of life. Grief, shame, illness, suffering, emotional paralysis—these are all ways we've been to the grave. But we have a liberating Lord who desires to open our graves and have us rise from them to life anew.

JOHN 11:3-7, 17, 20-27, 33B-45

The sisters of Lazarus sent word to Jesus saying, "Master, the one you love is ill." When Jesus heard this he said, "This illness is not to end in death, but is for the glory of God, that the Son of God may be glorified through it." Now Jesus loved Martha and her sister and Lazarus. So when he heard that he was ill, he remained for two days in the place where he was. Then after this he said to his disciples, "Let us go back to Judea."

When Jesus arrived, he found that Lazarus had already been in the tomb for four days. When Martha heard that Jesus was coming, she went to meet him; but Mary sat at home. Martha said to Jesus, "Lord, if you had been here, my brother would not have died. But even now I know that whatever you ask of God, God will give you." Jesus said to her, "Your brother will rise." Martha said to him, "I know he will rise, in the resurrection on the last day." Jesus told her, "I am the resurrection and the life; whoever believes in me, even if he dies, will live, and everyone who lives and believes in me will never die. Do you believe this?" She said to him, "Yes, Lord. I have come to believe that you are the Christ, the Son of God, the one who is coming into the world."

Jesus became perturbed and deeply troubled, and said, "Where have you laid him?" They said to him, "Sir, come and see." And Jesus wept. So the Jews said, "See how he loved him." But some of them said, "Could not the one who opened the eyes of the blind man have done something so that this man would not have died?"

So Jesus, perturbed again, came to the tomb. It was a cave, and a stone lay across it. Jesus said, "Take away the stone." Martha, the dead man's sister, said to him, "Lord, by now there will be a stench; he has been dead for four days." Jesus said to her, "Did I not tell you that if you believe you will see the glory of God?" So they took away the stone. And Jesus raised his eyes and said, "Father, I thank you for hearing me. I know that you always hear me; but because of the crowd here I have said this, that they may believe that you sent me." And when he had said this, he cried out in a loud voice, "Lazarus, come out!" The dead man came out, tied hand and foot with burial bands, and his face was wrapped in a cloth. So Jesus said to them, "Untie him and let him go."

Now many of the Jews who had come to Mary and seen what he had done began to believe in him.

We know the central sign of this text is Jesus' power to bring life from death. Yet the verses that seem to strike us most poignantly involve tears and love. When Jesus came to the tomb, the gospel writer states strikingly, "Jesus wept" (John 11:35). The writer wants us to know that these are tears that flow out of love: "Jesus loved Martha and her sister and Lazarus" (11:5). When he began to weep, the bystanders remarked, "See how he loved him" (11:36).

The tears of Jesus for his friend Lazarus express the full truth of the incarnation. Jesus is indeed the Word become flesh, immersed fully in our bodily humanity, sharing intimately in the heartache of the world. Jesus expresses his anguish fully because the only way beyond death and grief is through it.

Amid his weeping and impelled by his love, Jesus moves toward the tomb. Jesus fully understands the experiential truth of human life that the deeper the love, the deeper the grief. Yet Jesus also points to the supernatural truth that the same love that causes our grief is also the source of our hope. The love that makes us weep, that moves us to follow our loved ones to the grave, that rages at the ravages of mortality, helps us realize that love is stronger than death. This love beyond the grave is a spark of divine love within us. The love of God in Jesus moved him to weep, go to the tomb, call out to his friend, and free him from death's permanence.

Because Jesus is the love of God incarnate, he is "the resurrection and the life" (John 11:25). Those who live in him experience abundant life here and now as they hope for the fullness of life to come. Sustained by the love of Jesus, we can grieve with fierceness at the death of our loved ones and also hope mightily with confident conviction. For the one who came to the tomb weeping is the one who cried out in a loud voice, "Lazarus, come out!" (11:43).

MEDITATIO

Ponder these graveside Scriptures with a view toward the risen life to which we are called. During these final days of Lent, we are summoned forth from the tomb of darkness into the splendor of light.

- Ezekiel's prophecy helped the people of Israel trust in God again at a time in which they felt they were doomed. Without the hope-filled word of God, our lives would remain in the depths of despair. In what ways has God's word brought you out of a dark night into the dawn of faith?

- The raising of Lazarus is the last of the seven "signs" in John's Gospel revealing who Jesus truly is for the world. This scene seems to show Jesus at his most human and divine moments. What does it reveal to you about Jesus?

In what ways does this passage show the unity of Jesus' humanity and divinity?

- Martha and Mary are friends of Jesus, but their understanding of Jesus is incomplete. In what ways are these two sisters shown to be models for those who are coming to a deep faith, even in the face of doubts?

- Visualize Jesus weeping at the tomb of his beloved friend Lazarus, and stand with him in his moments of deep grief. Spend a few moments with this meditation, and ask yourself how it affects your relationship with him.

- Dying is not limited to the end of our physical existence. In human life, we start dying as soon as we are born. All those things that sap our strength, prick our pride, hurt our hearts, or arrest our arrogance are all little deaths. We die in installments each day. What dying have I experienced lately? What has it taught me about living?

ORATIO

After you've listened to what God has to say to you through these Scriptures, consider what you want to say to God in response. You might want to begin with these words:

Liberating Lord, sin confines my life within the prison of mortality, but your love frees me from the hopelessness of death. Stand by me throughout the many deaths of my life, and help me trust in the love that offers me abundant life.

Continue responding to God in prayer in the words that arise from your own experience with the Scriptures.

CONTEMPLATIO

⅄

When the words of prayer are no longer necessary or helpful, just rest silently in the loving arms of the One who gave you life. Repeat his words to you: "I am the resurrection and the life" (John 11:25). Trust that he will accompany you through the doorway of death.

OPERATIO

⅄

At the tomb of Lazarus, Jesus said, "Untie him and let him go" (John 11:44). These words echo the words of God in Egypt: "Let my people go" (Exodus 8:20). How can you help free someone who is bound in an experience of death (grief, failure, depression, despair)?

Palm Sunday of the Lord's Passion

LECTIO

Place a crucifix, cross, or palm branch before you as you read the texts to enhance your awareness of the Christ-centeredness of all Scripture. Ask the Holy Spirit to help you listen and respond to the *sacra pagina* as you reflect on the texts for the beginning of this Holy Week.

When you have quieted your external and internal distractions, dedicate this time for sacred conversation with God.

ISAIAH 50:4-7

The Lord GOD has given me
  a well-trained tongue,
that I might know how to speak to the weary
  a word that will rouse them.
Morning after morning
  he opens my ear that I may hear;
and I have not rebelled,
  have not turned back.
I gave my back to those who beat me,
  my cheeks to those who plucked my beard;
my face I did not shield
  from buffets and spitting.

The Lord GOD is my help,
    therefore I am not disgraced;
I have set my face like flint,
    knowing that I shall not be put to shame.

The Servant Songs (Isaiah 42:1-9; 49:1-7; 50:4-11; 52:13–53:12) are found in the latter part of Isaiah, written around the time of Israel's exile. This mysterious figure is chosen by God to take on the sin and suffering of others. The Servant seems to be a failure, experiencing shameful suffering, rejection, and an unjust death. Yet through his trials, he accomplishes the saving will of God, bringing life not only for God's people but for all the nations. As these four Servant Songs are read throughout Holy Week, we realize how profoundly they have shaped the ministry of Jesus and how effectively these texts find their fullest meaning in his passion.

This third song shows the Servant as being attentive to God's word. Every morning God opens his ears that he might hear anew. Only after listening can the Servant speak and act on behalf of the weary and the downtrodden. The Servant's obedient listening to God's word and working on behalf of the disadvantaged open him to ridicule and persecution. God's Servant is beaten and battered, but he does not counter with insult or violence. He accepts his role and never wavers, because he knows that his suffering is the result of obedient love.

The Servant's mission is not suffering itself, though it is fulfilled at the cost of great suffering. The mission is to hear and receive God's word, to assimilate it in all its depths, and then to act in response to that word. That redeeming response, expressed through the Servant's teaching, healing, and serving, will challenge power, greed, and privilege in ways that will create bitter torment and affliction.

After truly hearing this Servant Song, prepare to listen with the ears of your heart to the Passion of our Lord Jesus Christ according to Matthew.

MATTHEW 27:11-54

Jesus stood before the governor, Pontius Pilate, and he questioned him, "Are you the king of the Jews?" Jesus said, "You say so." And when he was accused by the chief priests and elders, he made no answer. Then Pilate said to him, "Do you not hear how many things they are testifying against you?" But he did not answer him one word, so that the governor was greatly amazed.

Now on the occasion of the feast the governor was accustomed to release to the crowd one prisoner whom they wished. And at that time they had a notorious prisoner called Barabbas. So when they had assembled, Pilate said to them, "Which one do you want me to release to you, Barabbas, or Jesus called Christ?" For he knew that it was out of envy that they had handed him over. While he was still seated on the bench, his wife sent him a message, "Have nothing to do with that righteous man. I suffered much in a dream today because of him." The chief priests and the elders persuaded the crowds to ask for Barabbas but to destroy Jesus. The governor said to them in reply, "Which of the two do you want me to release to you?" They answered, "Barabbas!" Pilate said to them, "Then what shall I do with Jesus called Christ?" They all said, "Let him be crucified!" But he said, "Why? What evil has he done?" They only shouted the louder, "Let him be crucified!" When Pilate saw that he was not succeeding at all, but that a riot was breaking out instead, he took water and washed his hands in the sight of the crowd, saying, "I am innocent of this man's blood. Look to it yourselves." And the whole people said in reply, "His blood be upon us and upon our children." Then he released Barabbas to them, but after he had Jesus scourged, he handed him over to be crucified.

Then the soldiers of the governor took Jesus inside the praetorium and gathered the whole cohort around him. They stripped off his clothes and threw a scarlet military cloak about him. Weaving a crown out of thorns, they placed it on his head, and a reed in his right hand. And kneeling before him, they mocked him, saying, "Hail, King of the Jews!" They spat upon him and took the reed and kept striking him on the head. And when they had mocked him, they stripped him of the cloak, dressed him in his own clothes, and led him off to crucify him.

As they were going out, they met a Cyrenian named Simon; this man they pressed into service to carry his cross.

And when they came to a place called Golgotha—which means Place of the Skull—they gave Jesus wine to drink mixed with gall. But when he had tasted it, he refused to drink. After they had crucified him, they divided his garments by casting lots; then they sat down and kept watch over him there. And they placed over his head the written charge against him: This is Jesus, the King of the Jews. Two revolutionaries were crucified with him, one on his right and the other on his left. Those passing by reviled him, shaking their heads and saying, "You who would destroy the temple and rebuild it in three days, save yourself, if you are the Son of God, and come down from the cross!" Likewise the chief priests with the scribes and elders mocked him and said, "He saved others; he cannot save himself. So he is the king of Israel! Let him come down from the cross now, and we will believe in him. He trusted in God; let him deliver him now if he wants him. For he said, 'I am the Son of God.'" The revolutionaries who were crucified with him also kept abusing him in the same way.

From noon onward, darkness came over the whole land until three in the afternoon. And about three o'clock Jesus cried out in a loud voice, "*Eli, Eli, lema sabachthani?*" which means, "My God, my God, why have you forsaken me?" Some of the bystanders who heard it said, "This one is calling for Elijah." Immediately one of them ran to get a sponge; he soaked it in wine, and putting it on a reed, gave it to him to drink. But the rest said, "Wait, let us see if Elijah comes to save him." But Jesus cried out again in a loud voice, and gave up his spirit.

[Here all kneel and pause for a short time.]

And behold, the veil of the sanctuary was torn in two from top to bottom. The earth quaked, rocks were split, tombs were opened, and the bodies of many saints who had fallen asleep were raised. And coming forth from their tombs after his resurrection, they entered the holy city and appeared to many. The centurion and the men with him who were keeping watch over Jesus feared greatly when they saw the earthquake and all that was happening, and they said, "Truly, this was the Son of God!"

After Jesus had listened to God's word throughout his life, assimilating that word in all its depth, he made his final journey to Jerusalem to face his passion and death. When Jesus entered the city, the crowd cut branches from the trees and waved them, singing hosannas in royal welcome. The chants, the welcome, and even the donkey indicate the coming of the Messiah in humility and peace. As the liturgy invites us to wave our palm branches and join in procession, we do so knowing that the understanding of the crowd in Jerusalem was shallow, as is the wisdom of the world today, and the hosannas will quickly turn to cries of "Crucify him!" (Mark 15:13).

The question that Pilate put to Jesus is the same in all four gospels: "Are you the king of the Jews?" Likewise, the response of Jesus is the same: "You say so" (Matthew 27:11; Mark 15:2; Luke 23:3; John 18:37). Jesus answers ambiguously, not fully claiming the title of king because of its exalted, political connotations, yet not denying the charge because his kingship is fundamental to his identity as Messiah. The response of Jesus indicates that Pilate has the words right but does not understand the meaning of his own question. The four gospels also agree on the charge that was hung on the cross: "Jesus, the King of the

Jews" (Matthew 27:37; Mark 15:26; Luke 23:38; John 19:19). The throne for this king will be the cross. He will govern by self-giving and reign by dying.

The royal title "king" carries a meaning in the gospel beyond anything that Pilate or the Roman soldiers could have imagined. On the cross hangs the King whom God will raise up and give the highest glory in the heavens. On the cross is the King of the new creation that is breaking into the world. On the cross is the King who will claim the hearts of believers from Jerusalem to the ends of the earth.

MEDITATIO

God has opened your ears, like those of his Servant, that you may hear his word. Now seek to assimilate these texts in all their depth so that you can respond to them with your life.

- The Servant in Isaiah's prophecy is a model for lectio divina. How do you make yourself available for God's word, morning after morning? What does God's Servant teach you about how to receive God's word into your life?

- Compare your experience of reflecting on the Passion account in the context of lectio divina and hearing the Passion proclaimed in the context of liturgy. What are the differences? In what ways does each enrich your discipleship?

- The gospel is filled with people of the Passion—Pilate, the religious leaders, Barabbas, Pilate's wife, the soldiers, Simon of Cyrene, the passersby, the two revolutionaries crucified with Jesus, and the centurion. If we are honest, we can identify in some way with each of them. Which character do you find easiest to identify with? Which do you find most difficult to relate to your life?

- Pilate acts neither as a noble judge nor as a brave leader, but washes his hands of the whole matter and refuses to take responsibility for what happens to Jesus. Compromise, peer pressure, dismissing the advice of his spouse, fear of losing upward social mobility—all of these led Pilate to hand Jesus over to be crucified. Which of these can forfeit your own discipleship?

- In what way am I like Pilate in preferring not to firmly decide one way or another about Jesus? In what ways does this realization challenge me during this Holy Week?

ORATIO

After reflecting on the meaning of these texts, respond to God in prayer:

Royal Servant of God, you heard your Father's word and responded with unflinching obedience. As I seek to follow in your footsteps, reign over my life from your glorious cross.

Pray to God in praise of Christ's glorious cross, in petition for the strength to follow Christ, in repentance for failing to follow God's word, or in thanksgiving for the insights you have received.

CONTEMPLATIO

Place yourself in the silent darkness at the foot of the cross of Jesus. If and when you are ready, make a choice to follow him as king of your life. Ask him to reign over your heart today.

OPERATIO

You are entering the church's most holy week. On Holy Thursday, you will gather with Christ at the sacrificial table of the new covenant. On Good Friday, you will tenderly kiss the wood of the cross. On Holy Saturday, you will wait at the tomb, and in the Easter Vigil, you will process with the light of Christ, gather at the font of baptism, and celebrate his risen presence by eating his body and drinking his blood in the Eucharist. Join with the church and walk with Jesus this week.

Chapter Four

Lectio Divina for Lent: Year B
First Sunday of Lent

LECTIO

人

Quiet your inner spirit and free yourself from the distractions of the day so that you can hear the word of God. Kiss the text as a sign of your reverence for sacred Scripture and your desire to receive its transforming message.

Begin reading when you feel ready to hear God's voice. Read this familiar text as if for the first time. Try not to bring your own presumptions to the text, but listen to God speaking to you anew.

GENESIS 9:8-15

God said to Noah and to his sons with him: "See, I am now establishing my covenant with you and your descendants after you and with every living creature that was with you: all the birds, and the various tame and wild animals that were with you and came out of the ark. I will establish my covenant with you, that never again shall all bodily creatures be destroyed by the waters of a flood; there shall not be another flood to devastate the earth." God added: "This is the sign that I am giving for all ages to come, of the covenant between me and you and every living creature with you: I set my bow in the clouds to serve as a sign of the covenant between me and the earth. When I bring clouds over the earth, and the bow appears in the clouds, I will recall the covenant I have made between me and you and all living beings, so that the waters shall never again become a flood to destroy all mortal beings."

The ancient story of the ark expresses God's power over the corrupting forces of sin. God delivers a remnant of humanity and the creatures of the earth out of the deluge of human sinfulness that threatens to plunge the world back into primeval chaos. Out of the waters, the merciful God brings forth a new and liberated earth. In the context of this primal account, God makes a cosmic, overarching promise, the first reference to "covenant" in the Bible. It is a covenant of care and protection, made unconditionally with all humanity in every generation and with all the living creatures of the earth. This committed pledge of God to stand for and with creation makes new life possible and offers undying hope for the future.

God designates the rainbow as the sign of the covenant between God and the earth. It is a reminder, both for God and for the creatures of the world, of God's solemn vow to care for creation, even in the midst of the consequences of human sin. This is God's unconditional yes to all of life, expressed by this multicolored but elusive bridge of light, which joins heaven and earth. Under the sign of the rainbow, we are gathered this Lent to hope in God's mercy and promises, and to respond as creatures made in God's image.

The New Testament writers and the church's early theologians realized that Noah's ark emerging from the flood is an important prototype of salvation. In baptism, as in the flood, the waters express destruction and death as much as they express renewed life. The baptismal font is both a tomb and a womb. We go into the waters, as into the flooded earth, and we are baptized into the death of Christ, drowned to the corrupting forces of sin. But coming out of the waters, we discover a new creation, the resurrection of Christ, a new beginning that can never be undone.

After considering the several layers of meaning within this text of Genesis, you are prepared to listen to this stark and crucial narrative from the beginning of the Gospel of Mark.

MARK 1:12-15

The Spirit drove Jesus out into the desert, and he remained in the desert for forty days, tempted by Satan. He was among wild beasts, and the angels ministered to him.

After John had been arrested, Jesus came to Galilee proclaiming the gospel of God: "This is the time of fulfillment. The kingdom of God is at hand. Repent, and believe in the gospel."

As Israel was liberated from slavery through the destructive waters and then moved into the desert, so Jesus, immediately following his baptism, trekked into the desert. As his Israelite ancestors were tested in the wilderness for forty years, Jesus spent forty days in this stark and barren space in preparation for his public life. For Israel, the desert was a place of God's revelation and promises as well as a place of temptations and failures. Jesus is alone with the Spirit of God and the spirit of evil. The presence of God and the forces of sin, the angelic and the beastly, compete within him. As this struggle persists throughout his life, from the desert to the cross, he will show himself as the most faithful of the Israelites.

Jesus comes out of the parched wilderness strengthened and ready, like a rainbow of hope for the world, bridging heaven and earth. As his saving ministry begins, he utters an announcement, a promise, and a call. First, Jesus announces that the long-awaited time has come. The time of God's fulfillment is now. Next, Jesus promises that God's reign is at hand. All the covenant pledges, even God's cosmic oath made to Noah, are ready to be accomplished.

Finally, Jesus calls his listeners to "repent, and believe in the gospel" (Mark 1:15). The human response to this climactic moment of salvation is twofold. Jesus calls us to "repent," literally to turn around, to change our minds and hearts. This repentance is both a turning away from whatever defaces the image of God in us and a turning toward the source of divine, creative love. Jesus also calls us to "believe" in this good news. The evidence of God's reign is not evident to all, but must be discerned through faith.

During Lent the church calls us to deliberately enter into an interior space of stark wilderness. This forty-day retreat enables us to look with greater clarity at the choices we need to make in order to live as a follower of Jesus. In this place of testing called Lent, we dwell with the wild beasts and the angels. Let us prove our faithfulness and allow God's Spirit to move us from the dry wilderness to the flowing water of baptismal life.

MEDITATIO

ᴧ

Consider what aspects of your life experiences are highlighted by the biblical texts. Allow the book of your life and the inspired Scriptures to dialogue so that you come to understand the significance of these readings for you as you enter this Lent.

- What have you discovered in your hearing of the story of Noah that you had not understood before? How can reading a text without a preconceived understanding help you uncover new meaning in Scripture?

- Why do you suppose God gave the rainbow as the sign of his covenant with all creation? What new appreciation has your reflection given to this symbol? Why is the rainbow a powerful symbol for the season of Lent?

- In what way does the account of Noah and the flood add to your understanding of baptism? What new wisdom are you discovering about baptism as you journey through this Lent?

- In what way are you experiencing Lent as a journey from the desert toward the font of baptism? In what ways do you hope your Lenten practices will lead you to the baptismal waters or prepare you to renew your baptism at Easter?

- Jesus spent forty days in the wilderness accompanied by wild beasts and ministering angels. Consider the spiritual presence of the "beastly" and the "angelic" that accompanies you through periods of trial. What disciplines do you wish to practice this Lent in order to turn away from the forces of sin and toward the presence of God?

ORATIO

Pray to God in response to what you have discovered within yourself from your listening and reflection. You may begin with these words:

Lord God, you are faithful to your creation and promise never to abandon what you have made. In your mercy, listen to my prayer and be present in my trials. Help me to repent, to turn to you, and believe in the good news you offer to the world in Jesus, your Son.

Continue to interact with God as one who knows you intimately, cares about you deeply, and accepts you unconditionally.

CONTEMPLATIO

Imaginatively place yourself in the presence of a rainbow. See its elusive array of colors and imagine that it bridges your life with God's life. Just be present with this image and allow it to infuse you with trust and confidence in God.

OPERATIO

Consider how God's word is calling you to faithfulness. What can you do during this week of Lent to grow in fidelity to God's call and to demonstrate your faithfulness in action?

Second Sunday of Lent

LECTIO

⋏

Prepare your space for encountering God's word by lighting a candle or placing another visible symbol in front of you. Call upon the same Holy Spirit who inspired the sacred writers to fill your heart and kindle in you the fire of divine love.

As you read, highlight, underline, circle, or mark up the reading as a tool for interacting with the text. You will find that these marks help you to be attentive to details and to remember the words during your encounter with God's word.

GENESIS 22:1-2, 9A, 10-13, 15-18

God put Abraham to the test. He called to him, "Abraham!" "Here I am!" he replied. Then God said: "Take your son Isaac, your only one, whom you love, and go to the land of Moriah. There you shall offer him up as a holocaust on a height that I will point out to you."

When they came to the place of which God had told him, Abraham built an altar there and arranged the wood on it. Then he reached out and took the knife to slaughter his son. But the LORD's messenger called to him from heaven, "Abraham, Abraham!" "Here I am!" he answered. "Do not lay your hand on the boy," said the messenger. "Do not do the least thing to him. I know now how devoted you are to God, since you did not withhold from me your own beloved son." As Abraham looked about, he spied a ram caught by its horns in the thicket. So he went and took the ram and offered it up as a holocaust in place of his son.

Again the LORD's messenger called to Abraham from heaven and said: "I swear by myself, declares the LORD, that because you acted as you did in not withholding from me your beloved son, I will bless you abundantly and make your descendants as countless as the stars of the sky and the sands of the seashore; your descendants shall take possession of the gates of their enemies, and in your descendants all the nations of the earth shall find blessing—all this because you obeyed my command."

Before God called Abraham to travel to the heights of Moriah, God had already brought Abraham on a long journey of many years that enabled Abraham to trust him completely. So when God called once more, Abraham again replied, "Here I am" (Genesis 22:1). Here was the most agonizing trial of all. Abraham was to take his only beloved son on the way that would lead to his sacrificial death. Isaac was the child of God's promise, the one in whom rested the hopes of Abraham and Sarah, the one from whom would come descendants as numerous as the stars. The account presents the unfathomable will of God, whose ways are mysterious, yet whose final word is always mercy and grace.

The traditional Jewish commentary on this passage, commonly called "the binding of Isaac," maintains that God already knew the faithful obedience of Abraham, but God gave him the opportunity to actually express his generosity and goodness. Abraham would surrender all his hope and his entire future into God's hands. In this way, Abraham would show himself to be like God, made in the divine image and likeness. For God, too, has surrendered his hope, his saving plan, the future he desires for the world, into the freedom of human persons. God takes the risk that Abraham will respond in obedience, while Abraham takes the risk that God will provide. Both God and Abraham are ready to trust each other.

The binding of Isaac gave God's people a model of complete obedience to God in times of testing, teaching them that God would always prove to be worthy of their trust. The followers of Jesus found hints of God's plan in this narrative as they sought to understand the mystery of Christ's sacrificial death.

After listening with the ear of your heart to this account of generous fidelity, you are ready to hear anew the gospel of Jesus. Trace the sign of the cross on your forehead, lips, and heart to prepare yourself to embrace God's word with your whole life.

Mark 9:2-10

Jesus took Peter, James, and John and led them up a high mountain apart by themselves. And he was transfigured before them, and his clothes became dazzling white, such as no fuller on earth could bleach them. Then Elijah appeared to them along with Moses, and they were conversing with Jesus. Then Peter said to Jesus in reply, "Rabbi, it is good that we are here! Let us make three tents: one for you, one for Moses, and one for Elijah." He hardly knew what to say, they were so terrified. Then a cloud came, casting a shadow over them; from the cloud came a voice, "This is my beloved Son. Listen to him." Suddenly, looking around, they no longer saw anyone but Jesus alone with them.

As they were coming down from the mountain, he charged them not to relate what they had seen to anyone, except when the Son of Man had risen from the dead. So they kept the matter to themselves, questioning what rising from the dead meant.

God's people often climb mountains in order to experience a divine manifestation. Abraham climbed to the summit of Moriah in response to God's agonizing test. Moses went up Mount Sinai to encounter the covenant-making God of Israel. Elijah went to that same mountain and heard God's whispering yet transforming voice. Here Jesus ascends a high mountain with his chosen disciples for a divine manifestation. He offers them a fleeting glimpse and encouraging insight into the fullness of the mystery veiled by his humanity. In the sight and understanding of his disciples, Jesus is transfigured from the gifted prophet they had come to know to the mystery of divine presence and power in their midst.

In response to the call up the mountain, God manifests himself in an overshadowing cloud. From Mount Sinai throughout the biblical narratives, the cloud was shown to be a symbol of God's presence with his people. The voice that comes from the cloud focuses on Jesus and echoes the words of God to Abraham. Like Isaac, the only beloved son of his father, Jesus is God's beloved Son, ready to be led wherever he is called to go.

Jesus and the Father are in loving communion, a divine unity so penetrating that it transforms the entire being of Jesus, radiating a dazzling light with a whiteness that the earth cannot produce.

The disciples are caught up in a holy and fascinating mystery that they cannot adequately articulate. The mystery must be contemplated rather than described. The Father urges them to "listen" to Jesus. As they continue the journey with Jesus to Jerusalem, they must listen in meditative trust. Later they will come to understand how the threads of God's saving plan are woven throughout the saving history of Abraham, Moses, and Elijah, and lead to the cross of Jesus.

MEDITATIO

These scenes on the mountain are presented in the liturgy for our meditation and contemplation. Consider how God is manifested to you in these sacred texts as you ponder and reflect on their revealing power.

- What did God really want when "God put Abraham to the test"? (Genesis 22:1). What does God want from you in times of trial that could be described as a test?

- Mount Moriah was identified in later tradition with the Temple mount in Jerusalem (2 Chronicles 3:1). What do you suppose this connection with Abraham teaches about the purpose and meaning of sacrificial worship in the Temple?

- Why did the early Christians turn to this text from Genesis for insights into the meaning of Christ's cross? What deeper understanding does it offer to you?

- Consider the emotional content of these two scenes. What feelings might Abraham and Isaac have experienced as they walked up the mountain together? What emotions might Peter, James, and John have experienced as they journeyed to the mountaintop with Jesus? What do you feel as you read these accounts?

- Transfigurations in our own lives might be described as those events in which our hearts are able to "see" a much fuller meaning than what our eyes can see. What are the transfigurations you have experienced? When have you come to appreciate that the world is charged with God's grandeur?

ORATIO

Use the images and emotions from your lectio and meditatio as the foundation of your prayerful response to God. Imagine the joyful gratitude of Abraham and Isaac, as well as that of Peter, James, and John, as they came down the mountain. You may begin your prayer with these words:

Father, I want to be able to entrust my life to you and to do what you ask of me. Give me the strength to always remain faithful to you and to trust your plan for my life. Help me to listen to Jesus as I take up the cross and follow in his way.

Continue voicing the prayer that issues from your heart as you ponder these scriptural scenes with gratitude.

CONTEMPLATIO

These narratives are filled with quiet awe. Sometimes we are incapable of expressing what we are experiencing. As the words of your prayer become inadequate to express your heart, just remain in silence before the majesty of God. Be assured that you can trust God completely through life's Lenten trials.

OPERATIO

How did God shape the faith of Abraham, Isaac, Peter, James, and John through these divine encounters? How is God shaping my faith through this encounter with God's word? How might God be challenging me to act on my renewed faith this week?

Third Sunday of Lent

LECTIO

Call upon the Holy Spirit to guide your listening to these sacred texts and to open your heart as you read. Vocalize the words of the text so that you not only read with your eyes but hear with your ears. Listen for the word of the Lord.

EXODUS 20:1-3, 7-8, 12-17

In those days, God delivered all these commandments:

"I, the LORD, am your God, who brought you out of the land of Egypt, that place of slavery. You shall not have other gods besides me.

"You shall not take the name of the LORD, your God, in vain. For the LORD will not leave unpunished the one who takes his name in vain.

"Remember to keep holy the sabbath day.

"Honor your father and your mother, that you may have a long life in the land which the LORD, your God, is giving you.

"You shall not kill.

"You shall not commit adultery.

"You shall not steal.

"You shall not bear false witness against your neighbor.

"You shall not covet your neighbor's house. You shall not covet your neighbor's wife, nor his male or female slave, nor his ox or ass, nor anything else that belongs to him."

The Ten Commandments, given by God to Moses on Mount Sinai, are prefaced by God's self-description: "I, the LORD, am your God, who brought you out of the land of Egypt, that place of slavery" (Exodus 20:2). The Israelites do not have to earn God's redemption by keeping the commandments. They are already redeemed through God's totally free act of love for his undeserving people. Obedience to the commandments, then, is a response to God's loving initiative in bringing his people to freedom.

The commandments are ten specific ways to respond faithfully, in single-hearted devotion, to our saving God. Rather than being means to earn God's favor, they are the ways to continue living in the freedom we have been given. With regard to God, they keep us away from the slavery of giving our lives to false gods and worshiping idols. They direct us to keep God alone at the center of our attention and to devote the Sabbath only to God. With regard to the community in which we live, obeying the commandments keeps us in just and loving relationships with family and society. They direct us to loving care of other people and to honest, committed relationships with parents, spouse, and neighbors. Distorted relationships with God or one another erode the freedom that we have been given through the covenant with our God.

After considering the fuller implications of this well-known text, realizing how it calls you to free and faithful living, you are ready to listen to the Gospel according to John. Read the text aloud and listen for the word of God with the ears of your heart.

JOHN 2:13-25

Since the Passover of the Jews was near, Jesus went up to Jerusalem. He found in the temple area those who sold oxen, sheep, and doves, as well as the money changers seated there. He made a whip out of cords and drove them all out of the temple area, with the sheep and oxen, and spilled the coins of the money changers and overturned their tables, and to those who sold doves he said, "Take these out of here, and stop making my Father's house a marketplace." His disciples recalled the words of Scripture, *Zeal for your house will consume me*. At this the Jews answered and said to him, "What sign can you show us for doing this?" Jesus answered and said to them, "Destroy this temple and in three days I will raise it up." The Jews said, "This temple has been under construction for forty-six years, and you will raise it up in three days?" But he was speaking about the temple of his body. Therefore, when he was raised from the dead, his disciples remembered that he had said this, and they came to believe the Scripture and the word Jesus had spoken.

While he was in Jerusalem for the feast of Passover, many began to believe in his name when they saw the signs he was doing. But Jesus would not trust himself to them because he knew them all, and did not need anyone to testify about human nature. He himself understood it well.

During the catechumenal period, the Ten Commandments have been a significant part of catechesis, and during this period of purification and enlightenment, they are an important means of self-examination and scrutiny. As we gather with the Elect and prepare for the renewing waters of baptism, we are called to scrutinize and cleanse the holy temple of our hearts. The gospel scene creates a vivid image of the kind of zeal that Jesus has for us and the desire he has to renew his risen life within us.

Throughout his life, Jesus lived in obedience to God's commandments and exemplified a free and faithful response to the covenant with God on Mount Sinai. The Torah for Jesus was not a dead code of ritual observance but the living word of Israel's liberating God. The prophetic action of Jesus in the Temple expresses his burning passion for returning Israel to the covenant with God, to making God's Temple truly his "Father's house," the place where God dwells with his people on earth.

The prophets of Israel had spoken of the messianic age, the time when the Temple would be cleansed of all actions and attitudes that were not worthy of it as the house of God. In this prophetic action, Jesus proclaims that the time of the Messiah was here, the time of fulfillment for the Torah and the prophets. By urging God's people and their leaders to return to the terms of the covenant God made with them at Mount Sinai, he is advocating a return to the heart of the matter. As stated in the gospel for this Sunday in Cycle A, Jesus was preparing for the time in which "true worshipers will worship the Father in Spirit and truth" (John 4:23).

Jesus' motivation for his prophetic action is expressed in a quotation from Psalm 69: "Zeal for your house will consume me" (verse 10). The double meaning contained in this verse when applied to Jesus offers us a deeper understanding of this scene. "House" refers both to the Temple and God's "household," the people of God. The zealous desire of Jesus that God dwell with his people and his zealous love for God's people not only fill Jesus but literally consume his life. This zeal for manifesting God's presence in the world will lead him to the cross. Yet the true place of God's dwelling is Jesus himself, the Temple that will be destroyed and then raised up in three days. As the Word of God enfleshed in the world, the risen Christ is the dwelling place of God among his people, the new and fullest access to the unseen God.

MEDITATIO

Reflect on these texts so that they may become a means of self-examination and scrutiny for you during this season of Lent. Consider how you can allow the printed text to become the living word of our liberating God.

- How does God's preface to the Ten Commandments place them in their proper context? What new understanding of obedience does this context offer to you?

- Why does the command to worship God alone come before the other commandments? What are the other gods that can limit and erode the freedom God has given to you?

- The quality of worship expresses the quality of one's relationship with God. How does Jesus' prophetic action in the Temple call God's people to true and grateful worship? How do you wish Jesus to cleanse your worship during this Lent?

- What is the difference between zeal for God and religious fanaticism? Who do you know that exemplifies an admirable zeal modeled on Jesus' passion for God?

- Jesus had a consuming love for the Father and a consuming desire that God dwell with his people. In what way can you live with consummate love for God and God's people this Lent?

ORATIO

Using the words, images, and emotions from the texts you have reflected upon, offer your response to God's word. You may begin your prayer with these words:

Liberating God of Israel, you have freed us from bondage to the enslaving forces of sin and evil and brought us into a covenant bond with you. Help me to live in fidelity to you and respond with loving obedience to the commands you have given to preserve my freedom.

Continue your prayer with words that convey the sentiments of your heart. Try to express your prayer with a zeal worthy of the God who liberates you from falsehood and distorted living.

CONTEMPLATIO

In light of the consuming love of Christ that led to his death for us, we can offer nothing in exchange or to merit that divine gift. Simply accept with gratitude the gift of God's redeeming grace.

OPERATIO

Choose one of the Ten Commandments and translate its prohibition into a positive command. Decide how you can live out that commandment in loving obedience this week.

Fourth Sunday of Lent

LECTIO

∧

Prepare your space for encountering God's living word in Scripture. Light a candle or place some other visible symbol before you to help you focus on the texts. Call upon the Holy Spirit to enlighten your eyes and your mind as you read the sacred Scriptures.

Begin reading when you are prepared to encounter God through the words of the *sacra pagina*.

2 CHRONICLES 36:14-16, 19-23

In those days, all the princes of Judah, the priests, and the people added infidelity to infidelity, practicing all the abominations of the nations and polluting the LORD's temple which he had consecrated in Jerusalem.

Early and often did the LORD, the God of their fathers, send his messengers to them, for he had compassion on his people and his dwelling place. But they mocked the messengers of God, despised his warnings, and scoffed at his prophets, until the anger of the LORD against his people was so inflamed that there was no remedy. Their enemies burnt the house of God, tore down the walls of Jerusalem, set all its palaces afire, and destroyed all its precious objects. Those who escaped the sword were carried captive to Babylon, where they became servants of the king of the Chaldeans and his sons until the kingdom of the Persians came to power. All this was to fulfill the word of the LORD spoken by Jeremiah: "Until the land has retrieved its lost sabbaths, during all the time it lies waste it shall have rest while seventy years are fulfilled."

In the first year of Cyrus, king of Persia, in order to fulfill the word of the LORD spoken by Jeremiah, the LORD inspired King Cyrus of Persia to issue this proclamation throughout his kingdom, both by word of mouth and in writing: "Thus says Cyrus, king of Persia: All the kingdoms of the earth the LORD, the God of heaven, has given to me, and he has also charged me to build him a house in Jerusalem, which is in Judah. Whoever, therefore, among you belongs to any part of his people, let him go up, and may his God be with him!"

The Hebrew writer describes the period of deep darkness that had fallen over the people of Israel. The Temple was defiled with corrupt practices, the prophets were ridiculed for speaking the word of God, and injustices filled the land with no sign of the people repenting. The cumulative effects of the evil perpetrated by the kings, priests, and people of the land led to the worst disaster imaginable as well as unspeakable suffering: the Temple was destroyed, Jerusalem was burned, priests were killed, and many were taken into exile by the Babylonians.

Yet out of this desperate situation, the good news of salvation was announced. Out of the darkness and suffering of exile arose a most unlikely rescuer for God's people. Cyrus, king of the Persians, decreed that the people were to be freed from exile and return to

Jerusalem. Cyrus charged them with rebuilding the Temple with the blessings of their God. This foreign king, ruler of the Persian empire, became God's improbable instrument of salvation. God's compassionate love for his people brought forth this unlikely liberator from his people's dark captivity.

This account tells the story of salvation in miniature. The situation goes from bad to worse. Infidelity reigns. Priests, prophets, and kings prove to be ineffective. Then, in the most improbable way, God's salvation dawns from the darkness. A savior arises, and the surprising, undeserved, unmerited rescue of God's people is achieved.

When you have absorbed God's pattern of redemption through this account of Israel's rescue from exile, prepare your mind for John's unlikely account of the Savior of the world.

JOHN 3:14-21

Jesus said to Nicodemus: "Just as Moses lifted up the serpent in the desert, so must the Son of Man be lifted up, so that everyone who believes in him may have eternal life."

For God so loved the world that he gave his only Son, so that everyone who believes in him might not perish but might have eternal life. For God did not send his Son into the world to condemn the world, but that the world might be saved through him. Whoever believes in him will not be condemned, but whoever does not believe has already been condemned, because he has not believed in the name of the only Son of God. And this is the verdict, that the light came into the world, but people preferred darkness to light, because their works were evil. For everyone who does wicked things hates the light and does not come toward the light, so that his works might not be exposed. But whoever lives the truth comes to the light, so that his works may be clearly seen as done in God.

Jesus presents himself in comparison to the bronze serpent of Israel's Exodus journey. When the people were dying from the bites of poisonous snakes in the desert, God told Moses to forge a serpent of bronze and raise it on a stake. All who gazed upon the uplifted serpent were restored to health (see Numbers 21:8-9). In commenting on this episode, the author of the Book of Wisdom described the brazen serpent lifted up on the stake as a "sign of salvation," saying to God, "He who turned toward it was saved, / not by what he saw, / but by you, the savior of all" (16:5-7).

A serpent mounted on a stake is a fearful and appalling sight. Yet this unlikely sign of salvation restored the health of God's people in the desert. Likewise, Jesus nailed to the cross is a gruesome spectacle. Yet when Jesus is lifted up on the cross, those who look upon him and believe will be forever healed and receive eternal life.

Like the improbable decree of Cyrus of Persia and the shocking serpent lifted up on the stake, God raised up Jesus on the cross as the instrument of the world's healing. From the midst of darkness and desperation, in paradoxical and unlikely ways, God brings the instrument of salvation to his people. The flesh of the Son of Man was senselessly twisted around the wood of the cross, forged by the fire of his passion and death, and raised up for the salvation of the world. In an astonishing divine paradox, the unjustly, senselessly crucified Jesus becomes the sign of salvation for all who are victims of the world's injustices, exiles, plagues, and brutalities.

Through the saving work of God, the cross was transformed from the world's most hated instrument of torture into the symbol of humanity's greatest hope. Into the distorted darkness and suffering of human history, God sent its most unlikely Savior: "For God so loved the world that he gave his only Son, so that everyone who believes in him might not perish but might have eternal life" (John 3:16).

As we gaze on this mystery of the uplifted Christ and contemplate the cross as the instrument of our salvation, our faith deepens and we experience the gift of eternal life.

The uplifted Christ that emerges from the darkness of the world's suffering is revealed as the Light that came into the world. We often prefer the darkness to the light, which exposes those aspects of ourselves that we would rather keep hidden. But during Lent, we seek to admit our sinful tendencies, expose them to ourselves and to God, and let Christ's light shine into the dark corners of our hearts to cast out the darkness. The wooden cross, which we raise on Good Friday, is illumined by the paschal candle of the Easter Vigil, from which we catch fire and rekindle our belief in the saving love with which God sent his only Son into the world for our eternal life.

MEDITATIO

Reflect on these Scriptures from the midst of your own darkness, confusion, suffering, and struggles. Consider God's saving work in your life and how during this Lent, you can accept the light of God's eternal life.

- In what ways do the Scriptures reveal King Cyrus of Persia, the bronze serpent on the stake, and the raised cross of Jesus as God's signs of salvation for his people? Why do you suppose God would reveal his saving love through such paradoxical signs?

- How do these Scriptures demonstrate that God's salvation is undeserved and unearned by God's people? How do you experience salvation as God's unmerited grace?

- In what ways is the uplifted bronze serpent a foreshadowing of the cross of Jesus? What fearful or appalling experience has become a source of healing or growth for you?

- Often people do not perceive the darkness that is around them and within them, and they mistake it for business as usual. In what ways does our world deny the darkness and cooperate with the deception? Why are people often so willing to become accomplices in this deceit of one another?

- In John's Gospel, eternal life does not refer to chronology but to the quality of life. It is a life that begins in the present and is perfected in eternity. In what ways do you experience God's eternal and abundant life today?

ORATIO

⅄

Offer to God what you have discovered in yourself from your meditation. Begin your prayer with these words and then continue in your own words:

Exalted Lord, you were lifted up on the cross so that whoever believes in you will not perish but have eternal life. As I gaze on your uplifted cross, deepen my faith in you and in your power to save me from the darkness of sin and death.

When the words of prayer begin to seem inadequate and no longer necessary, move into the wordless prayer of contemplatio.

CONTEMPLATIO

⅄

Gaze upon a candle flame, cross, or crucifix, or see the crucified Christ with your mind's eye. Let the light and power of God's saving sign penetrate your heart and deepen your belief. You do not need to say or do anything. Simply accept the grace God wishes you to receive.

OPERATIO

⅄

As you realize the darkness that is around you and within you, what can you do this week to challenge the world's deceit? Into what dark corner of your heart or your community can you let Christ's light shine?

Fifth Sunday of Lent

LECTIO

∧

Approach these texts with expectant faith, trusting that God wishes to transform your heart with the power of his word. When you are prepared, read these texts aloud, reading with your eyes and your lips and listening with your ears and your heart. Hear these inspired words in a new way, guided by God's renewing Spirit.

JEREMIAH 31:31-34

The days are coming, says the LORD, when I will make a new covenant with the house of Israel and the house of Judah. It will not be like the covenant I made with their fathers the day I took them by the hand to lead them forth from the land of Egypt; for they broke my covenant, and I had to show myself their master, says the LORD. But this is the covenant that I will make with the house of Israel after those days, says the LORD. I will place my law within them and write it upon their hearts; I will be their God, and they shall be my people. No longer will they have need to teach their friends and relatives how to know the LORD. All, from least to greatest, shall know me, says the LORD, for I will forgive their evildoing and remember their sin no more.

Jeremiah spoke these words of hope when God's people were empty of hope and filled with fear and despair. The Babylonians were threatening Israel, and the destruction of Jerusalem and its Temple was imminent. The people of the covenant wondered if God had deserted them and had forgotten the promises that had sustained their relationship.

The prophet's announcement of a new covenant between God and his people offers hope for the kind of intimate relationship God had always desired with Israel. This new covenant would not annul the earlier covenants with Noah, Abraham, Moses, and David. These divine pledges were really different moments in the history of the one great covenant between God and his people. Jeremiah's hope is for a renewed and more perfect expression of Israel's long-standing relationship with God.

As in Israel's former history, God again takes the initiative, promising his divine presence and pledging a heart-to-heart relationship. There will be no need to write the terms of the covenant on stone tablets because God's desire will be inscribed on his people's hearts. With merciful love, God will forgive and forget their sinfulness, giving them a renewed ability to respond faithfully to God. With deep empathy and renewed affection, God announces, "I will be their God, and they shall be my people" (Jeremiah 31:33).

Jesus is the climax of God's covenantal relationship with Israel, a bond intended from the beginning to eventually encompass all nations. Jesus incarnates God's forgiveness and covenant fidelity. In him all people can come to know God and experience God's will for humankind. On the cross, Jesus shed his blood for the forgiveness of sins, "the blood of the new and everlasting covenant," as the priest says in the Eucharistic prayers at Mass. The Eucharist is the sacrament of our ongoing relationship with God through Christ. As the ancient covenants with Israel were ratified and renewed with a sacrifice offered to God and by sharing in a sacred meal, so the Eucharist is our assurance of God's faithful promises and our ongoing commitment to be his people in Christ.

JOHN 12:20-33

Some Greeks who had come to worship at the Passover Feast came to Philip, who was from Bethsaida in Galilee, and asked him, "Sir, we would like to see Jesus." Philip went and told Andrew; then Andrew and Philip went and told Jesus. Jesus answered them, "The hour has come for the Son of Man to be glorified. Amen, amen, I say to you, unless a grain of wheat falls to the ground and dies, it remains just a grain of wheat; but if it dies, it produces much fruit. Whoever loves his life loses it, and whoever hates his life in this world will preserve it for eternal life. Whoever serves me must follow me, and where I am, there also will my servant be. The Father will honor whoever serves me.

"I am troubled now. Yet what should I say? 'Father, save me from this hour'? But it was for this purpose that I came to this hour. Father, glorify your name." Then a voice came from heaven, "I have glorified it and will glorify it again." The crowd there heard it and said it was thunder; but others said, "An angel has spoken to him." Jesus answered and said, "This voice did not come for my sake but for yours. Now is the time of judgment on this world; now the ruler of this world will be driven out. And when I am lifted up from the earth, I will draw everyone to myself." He said this indicating the kind of death he would die.

John's Gospel offers us a taste of the anguish and inner turmoil Jesus experienced while approaching his passion and death. Jesus' emotional expression and determination make this passage similar to the Gethsemane scene in the other three gospels. Jesus resists the temptation to ask the Father to save him from the hour of his passion, recognizing that it is for this reason that he has arrived at this hour. His whole life was oriented to reveal the Father's love that transforms human life through death. Instead of asking for rescue, Jesus says, "Father, glorify your name" (John 12:28), the equivalent of "Thy will be done" in the Gethsemane accounts. The whole of Jesus' ministry has been a revelation of the Father's glory, the glory that will again be manifested when Jesus is lifted up on the cross.

Until this hour of Jesus, sin and death had ruled in the world. The cross is the authority that defeats the powers of this world. In his death, Jesus will be "lifted up from the earth" (John 12:32). His death will not be extermination but exaltation. This transforming death of Jesus is the kind of death that will draw all people to him.

Jesus illuminates the path of his glorification with the image of the germinating grain of wheat. The grain that does nothing, that simply stays in the granary, slowly disintegrates, accomplishing nothing. But when it falls into the earth, it empties itself and dies. It is then that new life breaks forth from the husk, and it bears much fruit. This process of transformation through dying is the path of discipleship—death to self-centeredness, to the reign of sin, to the desire to protect our own security to the neglect of others. From grains of wheat, buried in the warm love and service of others and moistened by the living waters of our baptismal commitments, we grow into the mystery of the death and resurrection of Jesus. We are transformed and lifted up into a higher, abundant, and eternal life.

MEDITATIO

Each year the Lenten liturgy presents these readings for us to disturb our "business as usual" way of living. Consider the ways that taking these Scriptures to heart could result in a transformed way of life.

- A life lived under covenant is an exclusive way of life. God describes this relationship with his people: "I will be their God, and they shall be my people" (Jeremiah 31:33). In covenant God is our only God, and we must live the life that reflects his image. How is life in the new covenant challenging you to live this Lent?

- The Eucharist presents for us again the new covenant ratified in the sacrificial death of Jesus on the cross. In what ways is your understanding of the Eucharist enriched by understanding it as a covenant renewal and covenant commitment?

- There is a saying from the Sufi tradition that seems to describe the way of Jesus: "Die before you die so when you die, you won't die." What does this teaching mean for the way you wish to live?

- In what way does the image of the grain of wheat describe dying as a transformative process? In what ways must you "die" in order to follow the path of Jesus?

- What is it about the raised cross that draws people to Jesus? How are you drawn to the cross as Holy Week approaches?

ORATIO

After allowing yourself to be disturbed and challenged by these Scriptures, respond to God with the prayer that arises from your disturbance. Begin with these words, and allow them to spark your own words of prayer.

"Jesus, help me to surrender to you and let go of the passing attractions of this world. I want to give myself for others so that my life will bear fruit for your glory."

Continue to pour out your heart until words fail and no longer seem necessary.

CONTEMPLATIO

As you move into silent, contemplative prayer, choose a word, phrase, or image from the Scriptures to be your focus. Just rest in

God's presence, recalling and repeating the word, phrase, or image when you get distracted.

OPERATIO

Lectio divina moves us in the direction of a transformed life. Consider the thoughts that arose in your meditatio and the inner renewal that occurred in contemplatio. To what change of attitude or action has this process brought you?

Palm Sunday of the Lord's Passion

LECTIO

From the earliest days of the church, disciples of Jesus gathered at this time of year to retell the story of their Lord's passion and death. They wished to keep alive the memory of Jesus and to experience again, in word and sacrament, his sacrificial love.

Prepare yourself to read these sacred texts and to incorporate the meaning of his passion into your own discipleship. Ask the Holy Spirit to help you listen and respond to the *sacra pagina* as you reflect on the readings for the beginning of this Holy Week.

ISAIAH 50:4-7

The Lord GOD has given me
   a well-trained tongue,
that I might know how to speak to the weary
   a word that will rouse them.
Morning after morning
   he opens my ear that I may hear;
and I have not rebelled,
   have not turned back.
I gave my back to those who beat me,
   my cheeks to those who plucked my beard;

my face I did not shield
   from buffets and spitting.

The Lord GOD is my help,
   therefore I am not disgraced;
I have set my face like flint,
   knowing that I shall not be put to shame.

As the early Christians gathered to proclaim the Passion of Jesus Christ, there is no doubt that they included in their scriptural readings the messianic texts of the prophets, especially the Servant Songs of Isaiah (42:1-9; 49:1-7; 50:4-11; 52:13–53:12). These four texts, the third of which we hear today, were written around the time of Israel's exile. This mysterious figure is chosen by God to take on the sin and suffering of others. The Servant seems to be a failure, experiencing shameful suffering, rejection, and an unjust death. Yet through his trials, he accomplishes the saving will of God, bringing life not only for God's people but for all the nations.

While the precise historical identity of this Servant figure remains mysterious, the early Christians found in this figure a prototype of Jesus. These Servant texts have profoundly shaped the church's understanding of Jesus, and they find their fullest meaning in his passion. Like Jesus, the Servant endures mockery and persecution in carrying out his divinely appointed mission. Yet despite his sufferings, he remains obedient to what he has heard God speaking.

The Servant is also a model for the ideal practice of lectio divina. As today's text declared, every morning God opens his ears so that he might hear the Lord's word anew. The Servant hears and receives God's word, seeks to assimilate it in all its depths, and then acts in response to that word. Flowing from his meditative approach to Scripture, he is moved to speak and act on behalf of the weary and the downtrodden. The Servant's obedient listening to God's word and his work on behalf of the disadvantaged expose him to ridicule and persecution. Yet he remains true to his calling out of the conviction that "the Lord is my help" (Isaiah 50:7).

After truly hearing this Servant Song, prepare to listen with the ears of your heart to the Passion of our Lord Jesus Christ according to Mark.

MARK 15:1-39

As soon as morning came, the chief priests with the elders and the scribes, that is, the whole Sanhedrin, held a council. They bound Jesus, led him away, and handed him over to Pilate. Pilate questioned him, "Are you the king of the Jews?" He said to him in reply, "You say so." The chief priests accused him of many things. Again Pilate questioned him, "Have you no answer? See how many things they accuse you of." Jesus gave him no further answer, so that Pilate was amazed.

Now on the occasion of the feast he used to release to them one prisoner whom they requested. A man called Barabbas was then in prison along with the rebels who had committed murder in a rebellion. The crowd came forward and began to ask him to do for them as he was accustomed. Pilate answered, "Do you want me to release to you the king of the Jews?" For he knew that it was out of envy that the chief priests had handed him over. But the chief priests stirred up the crowd to have him release Barabbas for them instead. Pilate again said to them in reply, "Then what do you want me to do with the man you call the king of the Jews?" They shouted again, "Crucify him." Pilate said to them, "Why? What evil has he done?" They only shouted the louder, "Crucify him." So Pilate, wishing to satisfy the crowd, released Barabbas to them and, after he had Jesus scourged, handed him over to be crucified.

The soldiers led him away inside the palace, that is, the praetorium, and assembled the whole cohort. They clothed him in purple and, weaving a crown of thorns, placed it on him. They began to salute him with, "Hail, King of the Jews!" and kept striking his head with a reed and spitting upon him. They knelt before him in homage. And when they had mocked him, they stripped him of the purple cloak, dressed him in his own clothes, and led him out to crucify him.

They pressed into service a passer-by, Simon, a Cyrenian, who was coming in from the country, the father of Alexander and Rufus, to carry his cross.

They brought him to the place of Golgotha—which is translated Place of the Skull—. They gave him wine drugged with myrrh, but he did not take it. Then they crucified him and divided his garments by casting lots for them to see what each should take. It was nine o'clock in the morning when they crucified him. The inscription of the charge against him read, "The King of the Jews." With him they crucified two revolutionaries, one on his right and one on his left. Those passing by reviled him, shaking their heads and saying, "Aha! You who would destroy the temple and rebuild it in three days, save yourself by coming down from the cross." Likewise the chief priests, with the scribes, mocked him among themselves and said, "He saved others; he cannot save himself. Let the Christ, the King of Israel, come down now from the cross that we may see and believe." Those who were crucified with him also kept abusing him.

At noon darkness came over the whole land until three in the afternoon. And at three o'clock Jesus cried out in a loud voice, "*Eloi, Eloi, lema sabachthani?*" which is translated, "My God, my God, why have you forsaken me?" Some of the bystanders who heard it said, "Look, he is calling Elijah." One of them ran, soaked a sponge with wine, put it on a reed and gave it to him to drink saying, "Wait, let us see if Elijah comes to take him down." Jesus gave a loud cry and breathed his last.

[Here all kneel and pause for a short time.]

The veil of the sanctuary was torn in two from top to bottom. When the centurion who stood facing him saw how he breathed his last he said, "Truly this man was the Son of God!"

As far as we know, Mark's Gospel contains the earliest written Passion account of Jesus. His gospel gives us the framework of the church's Holy Week celebration, beginning with the entrance of Jesus into Jerusalem as the humble and suffering Messiah, and ending with his death on the cross and entombment. Since Mark's Passion account is so climactic and important in the gospel's overall plan, Mark's entire gospel has been described as a Passion narrative with a long introduction. Throughout his gospel, Mark shows that Jesus' identity as teacher, healer, and Messiah can be properly understood only in light of the cross.

Contemplating the Passion of Jesus should make us somewhat uncomfortable. After all, it speaks about dimensions of the human situation that are terrifying: hatred, fear, injustice, misunderstanding, and innocent suffering. It shows us what sacrifice and selflessness are needed to overcome these terrible realities. The Passion shows us a God who seems to be helpless, refusing to intervene and cancel the horrible consequences of human choice and destructive deeds. We see a Messiah who not only humbles himself to ride into Jerusalem on a donkey, but who refuses to save himself and come down from the cross.

Jesus' agonizing Passion proceeds relentlessly. At 9 a.m. Jesus is nailed to the cross. At noon darkness falls over the whole land as witness to the cosmic tragedy of Jesus' crucifixion. At 3 p.m. the parched lips of Jesus cry out the desperate words, preserved in his native Aramaic, "My God, my God, why have you forsaken me?" (Mark 15:34). With the opening words of Psalm 22, Jesus begins to pray that great psalm of lament. Readers familiar with the Scriptures of Israel know that what seems to be a cry of despair is the beginning of a prayerful struggle that ends in triumphant hope.

The climax of Mark's Passion account, and indeed of his whole gospel, is the cry of the Roman centurion who looks upon the cross of the tortured and lifeless Christ: "Truly this man was the Son of God!" (Mark 15:39). Only in looking on the cross can anyone really understand Jesus and the meaning of his life. The cross is not a doctrine we can convincingly explain or a fact we can logically understand. It is ultimately a mystery to be contemplated. It is the truth of divine love made flesh and spent to the end.

MEDITATIO

Having listened to the inspired texts of Isaiah and Mark's Passion account, allow the Scriptures to interact with your own Lenten journey over these past weeks. Consider what personal messages and challenges these texts are offering to you.

- The Suffering Servant of Isaiah is a model for hearing, meditating, contemplating, and acting on God's word. Which aspects of the Servant's assimilation of the word of God resonate with your experience of lectio divina during this Lent?

- What aspects of the Passion account seem terrifying to you? What aspects seem comforting?

- Imagine the response of Barabbas as he watched Jesus being condemned and crucified in place of himself. What might have been some of his thoughts and feelings at the cross of Jesus?

- Who has been a Simon the Cyrenian for you, carrying the cross for part of your journey? How can you be a Simon for someone else?

- When have you felt abandoned? How can it help you to know that Jesus experienced abandonment from his friends and felt abandoned by God?

ORATIO

In response to Mark's Passion account, pray the words of Psalm 22, the words that Jesus prayed from the cross. Pray them with Jesus, allowing them to become your own prayer of lament and hope.

Continue praying in your own words, using some of the words, thoughts, and images of Isaiah, the psalmist, and Mark's Gospel.

CONTEMPLATIO

Choose one word from your oratio to bring into the silence of contemplatio. Focus on that word and allow God to work deeply within you, transforming you into a more complete divine image.

OPERATIO

The entire liturgical year of the church is focused on the paschal mystery of Christ celebrated during the days of the holy Triduum. On Holy Thursday, you will gather with Christ at the sacrificial table of the new covenant. On Good Friday, you will tenderly kiss the wood of the cross. On Holy Saturday, you will wait at the tomb, and in the Easter Vigil, you will process with the light of Christ, gather at the font of baptism, and celebrate his risen presence by eating his body and drinking his blood in the Eucharist. Join with the church and walk with Jesus this week.

Chapter Five

Lectio Divina for Lent: Year C

First Sunday of Lent

LECTIO

Open your heart to the Spirit of God. Ask the Holy Spirit to lead you through this lectio divina, to guide your understanding, to enkindle within you the fire of divine love.

Begin reading when you feel ready to hear God's voice speaking in Scripture. Slowly articulate the words so that you can listen better as you read.

DEUTERONOMY 26:4-10

Moses spoke to the people, saying: "The priest shall receive the basket from you and shall set it in front of the altar of the LORD, your God. Then you shall declare before the LORD, your God, 'My father was a wandering Aramean who went down to Egypt with a small household and lived there as an alien. But there he became a nation great, strong, and numerous. When the Egyptians maltreated and oppressed us, imposing hard labor upon us, we cried to the LORD, the God of our fathers, and he heard our cry and saw our affliction, our toil, and our oppression. He brought us out of Egypt with his strong hand and outstretched arm, with terrifying power, with signs and wonders; and bringing us into this country, he gave us this land flowing with milk and honey. Therefore, I have now brought you the firstfruits of the products of the soil which you, O Lord, have given me.' And having set them before the Lord, your God, you shall bow down in his presence."

The text describes the offering of the first fruits of the land as prescribed by the Torah. Each year the people of Israel would bring the earliest yield of their farming to the sanctuary in a gesture of thanksgiving to God. They would present their basketful of produce to the priest, who would set it before God's altar as a ritual offering.

Within this ritualized service, the Israelites would recite a summary of their experience of God as a people, which served as a kind of liturgical creed. This summary begins by recalling the lives of the fathers and mothers of Israel, who were nomads within the land. Jacob and his family went to Egypt to escape a famine, and there they grew into a populous people over several centuries. When they began to be oppressed with slavery and hard labor, God "heard" their cries of pain, "saw" their affliction, and rescued them from their bondage. God then enabled them to enter a good and productive territory, the land promised by God to their ancestors. So when Israelites professed their faith, they expressed their memory of suffering, their liberation by God's power, and the blessings they received in the land. There is no claim to special privilege before God. All is God's gift, bestowed on those who cry out to him in need.

The offering of first fruits to God acknowledges God as both Creator and Redeemer. As Creator, God made the earth and sustains its power to produce vegetation and food; as Redeemer, God freed his people from slavery and brought them into a land where they could live in freedom. In this ritual, through both words and deeds, God is praised as both the God of nature and the Lord of history. As such, God's people are able to trust God and live gratefully in his grace.

After making this word of God your own, begin reading the gospel when you are ready. Read this familiar account as if for the first time. Listen with expectation, confident that God will teach you something new through the words of the Gospel according to Luke.

Luke 4:1-13

Filled with the Holy Spirit, Jesus returned from the Jordan and was led by the Spirit into the desert for forty days, to be tempted by the devil. He ate nothing during those days, and when they were over he was hungry. The devil said to him, "If you are the Son of God, command this stone to become bread." Jesus answered him, "It is written, *One does not live on bread alone.*" Then he took him up and showed him all the kingdoms of the world in a single instant. The devil said to him, "I shall give to you all this power and glory; for it has been handed over to me, and I may give it to whomever I wish. All this will be yours, if you worship me." Jesus said to him in reply, "It is written:

You shall worship the Lord, your God,
 and him alone shall you serve."

Then he led him to Jerusalem, made him stand on the parapet of the temple, and said to him, "If you are the Son of God, throw yourself down from here, for it is written:

He will command his angels concerning you, to guard you,

and:

With their hands they will support you,
 lest you dash your foot against a stone."

Jesus said to him in reply, "It also says, *You shall not put the Lord, your God, to the test.*" When the devil had finished every temptation, he departed from him for a time.

The gospel text keeps us within the tradition of the Book of Deuteronomy, which narrates Israel's forty-year journey through the desert in search of the promised land. Luke presents us with a forty-day recap of Israel's epic trial with the testing of Jesus in the desert. Each of the responses offered by Jesus to his temptations is a quotation from Deuteronomy and a reflection of what his Israelite ancestors learned through their struggles. We might say that Jesus relives the experience of the Israelites in the wilderness, but he does it right.

This testing narrative reveals the steadfast heart of Jesus, just as the testing of ancient Israel revealed their obstinate hearts. The temptations focus on the messianic identity of Jesus, revealing faulty ways of thinking about his mission and how to carry it out. His first temptation is to see himself as a wonder-worker, catering to people's insistent demands. Though Jesus shows consistent care for people's needs, he does not win them over by miracles but calls them to a change of heart. The second temptation is to advance his identity by seeking political and religious power over other people. But Jesus will bring God's kingdom, not through the tactics of temporal control and influence, but through conversion and forgiveness. The third temptation is to win over people through some spectacular proof that he is the Messiah. But Jesus knows that people's lust for certitude can never be satisfied. Even from the cross, Jesus is taunted and dared by the onlookers to come down as proof that he is God's Son.

The devil did his best to seduce Jesus with strategies that would seem to further his messianic ambition. Yet Jesus saw through each of them, and he refused them, declining the tempting offers to betray his identity. He proved himself to be God's faithful one, with steadfast dedication to his mission and love for his people. During this season of Lent, we, too, are tested for forty days. Will we refuse the temptations to betray our Christian identity?

MEDITATIO

Spend some time reflecting on these two Scriptures, which recall Israel's wanderings in the wilderness. Considering your own sojourn of Lent, seek the meaning of these texts for your own journey of discipleship.

- What percentage of your food, labor, income, and time do you give away? What is the spiritual value in giving away our first fruits? Are there any ways you would like to practice offering your first fruits to God during Lent?

- The ancient Israelites professed their beliefs in a nutshell every time they offered their gifts at God's altar. How would you express the core of your experience of God in a brief statement or faith profession?

- The offering of first fruits expressed trust in the God who always provides. In the desert, Jesus expressed the trust that would maintain him throughout his life, even to the cross. How do you express trust in God?

- Jesus knew the Scriptures well and was able to recall verses that strengthened him as he refused the temptations to betray his identity. What verses of Scripture might help you when your identity as a Christian is challenged?

- Scripture teaches us that we are powerless to overcome temptation and sin on our own. Jesus shows us how to rely on the word and the power of God. How can you surrender your temptations to Christ and trust in the saving power of his cross?

ORATIO

Cry out to God in the midst of your trial and testing, knowing that he has conquered sin in his Son, Jesus. Trust in his power to overcome the evil tendencies to deny your God-given identity. Begin to pray in these words:

I cry out to you, creating and redeeming God. Through your grace, you have made me your child and a disciple of your Son, Jesus. Give me the strength to live faithfully in the identity you have given to me.

Continue praying from your heart in the words God's Spirit gives you.

CONTEMPLATIO

Be aware of the presence of God and offer yourself to him with trusting confidence. Claim the identity God has given you, and let God reinforce his image within you as you rest in wordless silence.

OPERATIO

Consider how God is molding and shaping you through this experience of lectio divina. How is your mind or heart different after having prayerfully reflected on these Lenten narratives? What does God want from you during this week of Lent?

Second Sunday of Lent

LECTIO

Close off the day's distractions and enter a quiet time for these moments with God's inspired word. Become aware of your breath as a gift of God, breathing in as you are filled with the presence of God and breathing out as you let go of all unnecessary anxiety.

Begin reading when you feel ready to hear God's voice in the sacred text.

GENESIS 15:5-12, 17-18

The Lord God took Abram outside and said, "Look up at the sky and count the stars, if you can. Just so," he added, "shall your descendants be." Abram put his faith in the LORD, who credited it to him as an act of righteousness.

He then said to him, "I am the LORD who brought you from Ur of the Chaldeans to give you this land as a possession." "O Lord GOD," he asked, "how am I to know that I shall possess it?" He answered him, "Bring me a three-year-old heifer, a three-year-old she-goat, a three-year-old ram, a turtledove, and a young pigeon." Abram brought him all these, split them in two, and placed each half opposite the other; but the birds he did not cut up. Birds of prey swooped down on the carcasses, but Abram stayed with them. As the sun was about to set, a trance fell upon Abram, and a deep, terrifying darkness enveloped him.

When the sun had set and it was dark, there appeared a smoking fire pot and a flaming torch, which passed between those pieces. It was on that occasion that the LORD made a covenant with Abram, saying: "To your descendants I give this land, from the Wadi of Egypt to the Great River, the Euphrates."

God's covenant with Abram (later called Abraham) is a pledge of abundance coming from scarcity, fertility from sterility. To the barren Abraham and Sarah, God promised descendants more numerous than the stars in the sky. To this nomadic couple, God assured that their progeny would possess a wide and bountiful land.

Covenants were common in the ancient world for defining and sealing various types of relationships and agreements. The covenant between God and Abraham contained the basic elements of ancient covenants: the identification of the one initiating the covenant, a statement of the history of the two parties entering the covenant, the blessings provided through the relationship, and the ceremony of ratifying the covenant.

In this mysterious ritual of covenant ratification, the animals to be sacrificed are cut in two, and the one making the covenant passes between the pieces to solemnly seal the covenant. The ritual expresses the conviction that the parties will suffer the same fate as the animals should they fail to keep the covenant (see Jeremiah 34:18). Here God, represented by the flaming torch and smoke, passes between the sundered animals, making a unilateral, unconditional covenant with Abram.

The promise of descendants and abundant land is God's gift, not a possession that Abraham could possibly deserve or earn from God. Abraham responded to God with faith. He put his faith in the Lord, who credited it to him as an act of righteousness (see Romans 4:3). Faith is not defined here; rather, we are shown what faith is through the example of Abraham. He put his full trust in God, even when that trust seemed unwarranted, and thus became the model of faith for us all.

After listening to this ancient account of God's covenant-making, prepare to hear this gospel account of Jesus, the Lord of God's new covenant. Notice the ways Luke demonstrates the unity between the old covenant with Israel and the new covenant in Christ.

Luke 9:28b-36

Jesus took Peter, John, and James and went up the mountain to pray. While he was praying his face changed in appearance and his clothing became dazzling white. And behold, two men were conversing with him, Moses and Elijah, who appeared in glory and spoke of his exodus that he was going to accomplish in Jerusalem. Peter and his companions had been overcome by sleep, but becoming fully awake, they saw his glory and the two men standing with him. As they were about to part from him, Peter said to Jesus, "Master, it is good that we are here; let us make three tents, one for you, one for Moses, and one for Elijah." But he did not know what he was saying. While he was still speaking, a cloud came and cast a shadow over them, and they became frightened when they entered the cloud. Then from the cloud came a voice that said, "This is my chosen Son; listen to him." After the voice had spoken, Jesus was found alone. They fell silent and did not at that time tell anyone what they had seen.

Each year, on the Second Sunday of Lent, the church proclaims the gospel of the transfiguration, either from Matthew, Mark, or Luke, depending on the liturgical cycle. These three accounts are very similar, but Luke's Gospel contains some unique elements that are not included in the others. Paying attention to these distinctive components of the text will help us understand Luke's insights into this glorious gospel scene.

First, Luke notes that Jesus took his disciples up the mountain to pray, and that he was transfigured "while he was praying" (Luke 9:29). According to the ancient view of the cosmos, God dwelt above the heavens, so praying on a mountain expressed the human effort to draw near to God. The cloud that covers the mountain from which the divine voice speaks, in turn, expresses God's descent. Prayer, then, is the process of both the ascending human and the descending divine, expressing the combination of human effort and divine grace.

Though this geographical symbolism of prayer helps us somewhat to understand the dynamic of prayer, it does not express the essence of Jesus' prayer. As he prays, Jesus is connected to God interiorly, in the deepest part of his being. His union with God becomes so complete that he becomes transparent to God. The divine presence radiates from his interior, illuminating his face and causing his garments to glow.

The second distinctive element of Luke's account is the subject of the conversation between Jesus, Moses, and Elijah. The text tells us that they "spoke of his exodus that he was going to accomplish in Jerusalem" (Luke 9:31). The events to come in Jerusalem, including the crucifixion and death of Jesus, are described as his exodus, the biblical term for the central event of Israel's relationship with God. As the Israelites journeyed from bondage to freedom, so Jesus' paschal mystery will be a new exodus for God's people. What seems to be a pending disaster will become a liberating event of which the first exodus is a foreshadowing. This exodus of Jesus is the fulfillment of God's saving plan, a plan that began with Abraham and the covenant, which continued in the exodus struggles of Moses, and was strengthened through the prophetic ministry of Elijah.

This discussion of Jesus' divine mission in Jerusalem shows us that the prayer of Jesus does not lead only to contemplatio but continues also in operatio. Though the three figures are on the mountain, they are considering the next step on the earth. The luminous Jesus, transparent to God and permeated with the divine presence, is the same Jesus who will stretch out his arms on the cross and die in surrender to divine love. The prayer on the mountain is preparation for the culminating mission of Jesus in Jerusalem.

MEDITATIO

God's voice told the disciples to "listen" to Jesus, a process that requires a silent and receptive mind. They had to learn how to temporarily suspend their own assumptions and let go of some of their mental defenses in order to truly learn from him. Spend some time reflecting on these biblical scenes until you are led to understanding.

- Abraham put his full trust in God, even when that trust seemed unwarranted, and thus became a model of faith for all who came after him. How is Abraham an example of faith in the circumstances of life which you now face?

- God promised countless descendants and abundant land to Abraham. What are the promises God has offered to you? In what way does your confidence in God give hope to your life?

- Faith is often a matter of seeing things in a way that is not universally shared. In what ways do these two readings illustrate this aspect of faith for you?

- In Luke's account, Moses and Elijah spoke to Jesus about "his exodus that he was going to accomplish in Jerusalem" (Luke 9:31). Why does Luke's Gospel describe the saving events of Christ's passion as "his exodus"? Why do you suppose the text emphasizes that this saving event was discussed by Moses and Elijah?

- In what way do the images of the transfiguration describe prayer as a combination of human effort and divine grace? In what ways do you experience prayer as a joining of effort and grace?

ORATIO

⋏

Prayer begins by listening to God's word with a receptive mind, followed by meditation on that word until the truth of that word leads to real understanding. When you are ready to respond to God's word with the words of your own prayer, you might begin like this:

God of Abraham, Moses, and Elijah, you are the source of all that I am and all that I have. Help me to trust completely in you, even when your promises to me seem distant and doubtful. Open my heart to truly listen to your Son so that I can understand your inspired word.

Ask God to help you trust in him completely.

CONTEMPLATIO

⋏

Imagine the cloud of God's presence overshadowing you on the mountaintop. Rest in that image, and experience the divine presence surrounding you. Spend some quiet moments allowing God to be present in your innermost being.

OPERATIO

⋏

The disciples descended the mountain with Jesus in order to travel with him to Jerusalem. In what ways has your prayerful listening to these Scriptures helped prepare you for the work of following Jesus to the cross?

Third Sunday of Lent

LECTIO

⅄

Light a candle or place some other symbol before you to focus your attention. As Moses removed his sandals because the place where he stood was holy ground, remove from your mind and heart whatever hinders you from receiving God's word. Vocalize the words of the text so that you not only read with your eyes but hear with your ears.

EXODUS 3:1-8A, 13-15

Moses was tending the flock of his father-in-law Jethro, the priest of Midian. Leading the flock across the desert, he came to Horeb, the mountain of God. There an angel of the LORD appeared to Moses in fire flaming out of a bush. As he looked on, he was surprised to see that the bush, though on fire, was not consumed. So Moses decided, "I must go over to look at this remarkable sight, and see why the bush is not burned."

When the LORD saw him coming over to look at it more closely, God called out to him from the bush, "Moses! Moses!" He answered, "Here I am." God said, "Come no nearer! Remove the sandals from your feet, for the place where you stand is holy ground. I am the God of your fathers," he continued, "the God of Abraham, the God of Isaac, the God of Jacob." Moses hid his face, for he was afraid to look at God. But the LORD said, "I have witnessed the affliction of my people in Egypt and have heard their cry of complaint against their slave drivers, so I know well what they are suffering. Therefore I have come down to rescue them from the hands of the Egyptians and lead them out of that land into a good and spacious land, a land flowing with milk and honey."

Moses said to God, "But when I go to the Israelites and say to them, 'The God of your fathers has sent me to you,' if they ask me, 'What is his name?' what am I to tell them?" God replied, "I am who am." Then he added, "This is what you shall tell the Israelites: I AM sent me to you."

God spoke further to Moses, "Thus shall you say to the Israelites: The LORD, the God of your fathers, the God of Abraham, the God of Isaac, the God of Jacob, has sent me to you.

"This is my name forever;
thus am I to be remembered through all generations."

The desert, the mountain, and fire are the material elements through which God manifests himself to Moses. The desert forms the solitary sanctuary in which Moses hears God's voice. Here the Israelites would be led by Moses in a forty-year retreat to be bonded with God. The mountain, mysteriously reaching into the clouds, represents human ascending and divine descending to communicate. Here the Israelites would encounter God and become his own people. Fire, both fascinating and terrifying, evokes God's holiness, mystery, and passion. Just as fire is always flickering and changing its shape, refusing to be held for examination, so is God always indefinable and beyond human grasp. The paradox of the fire that burns the bush without consuming it expresses the divine presence within the material world, the presence of God that can be intense as well as intimate without violating the distinct essence of the creature.

In the ancient world, a name expressed one's true nature. To know a divine name meant that one could call on the presence of the deity and create a relationship. Without a name, a god remained a distant, impersonal force. For Israel the gift of God's name was a revelation of the divine Person. Yet God reveals himself to Israel through what he does in history. God is not static or unresponsive. God's truest nature is revealed through the divine action of overthrowing oppressors and calling Israel to a new life characterized by freedom.

God's name is more of a verb than a noun, a form of the verb "to be." It expresses the freedom of God to be present wherever and whenever God wills. The presence and the power of "I AM" cannot be captured or controlled by building a temple, creating an idol, or invoking the right name, as was possible with the gods of other peoples. God's name could only be understood as its meaning unfolded in Israel's own historical experiences of God's dynamic presence with them.

The only human response to such a God is trust. Yet for God's people, this trust was based on the assuring experiences of the past. The God made known to Abraham, Isaac, and Jacob is the God who is revealed to Moses as the trustworthy God who plans to bring his people to freedom.

After grappling to understand this text of God's revelation to Moses, turn to the gospel passage. Here Jesus, too, teaches us to trust in this God, who has been faithful throughout history yet who challenges us to be obedient in the present.

LUKE 13:1-9

Some people told Jesus about the Galileans whose blood Pilate had mingled with the blood of their sacrifices. Jesus said to them in reply, "Do you think that because these Galileans suffered in this way they were greater sinners than all other Galileans? By no means! But I tell you, if you do not repent, you will all perish as they did! Or those eighteen people who were killed when the tower at Siloam fell on them—do you think they were more guilty than everyone else who lived in Jerusalem? By no means! But I tell you, if you do not repent, you will all perish as they did!"

And he told them this parable: "There once was a person who had a fig tree planted in his orchard, and when he came in search of fruit on it but found none, he said to the gardener, 'For three years now I have come in search of fruit on this fig tree but have found none. So cut it down. Why should it exhaust the soil?' He said to him in reply, 'Sir, leave it for this year also, and I shall cultivate the ground around it and fertilize it; it may bear fruit in the future. If not you can cut it down.'"

As the God revealed to Moses is both fascinating and fearful, those same qualities of attractiveness and awesomeness are present in the God revealed by Jesus. While the Exodus text offered the image of the burning bush, unconsumed by the revealing flame, the gospel draws on another image for the divine and human interaction: the fruitless fig tree. A tree meant to be fruitful is in danger of being cut down. In its unfruitful state, it is wasting the soil. Like the fig tree, we are called to bear fruit, to fulfill our mission of doing the will of God on earth. The fearful possibility of perishing without producing must compel us to repentance.

Jesus' parable of the fig tree is initiated by the report of two disasters offered by those listening to Jesus. The first recounts a horrible incident in which some Galileans were visiting Jerusalem to offer sacrifices in the Temple. Pilate sent in troops and murdered the Galileans, thus mingling their blood with that of their sacrifices. The second relates an accidental event in which a tower fell in Jerusalem, killing eighteen people. The crowd wants to know if these events, one caused by human violence and the other a natural disaster, were somehow connected to God's will and if they were punishment for sin. The response of Jesus is an emphatic no to this way of thinking.

Instead of offering philosophical speculation about why bad things happen to good people, as so many have attempted to do through the ages, Jesus uses the reports of disaster to call his listeners to a far more urgent matter. Jesus says that unless they repent, they, too, will all likewise perish. While speculating about the fate of others, they are suddenly confronted with their own fate—a destiny not dependent on the whim of Pilate or shifting platelets in the earth below Jerusalem, but reliant on their own choices. Rather than looking outside of themselves in abstract conjecture about others, people must look inside themselves to experience God's will and then activate that will in the events of their lives.

God's will is that we change our hearts, that we repent and bear fruit. Doing God's will "on earth as it is in heaven" (see Matthew 6:10) means bringing God's compassionate and healing presence into the world in which we live. This is what it means to bear fruit. If our fig tree is currently without fruit, Lent is the time to allow the divine Gardener to till the ground around us, loosen up our roots, fertilize regularly, and water plentifully.

MEDITATIO

Allow the renewing power of God's word to work within you, calling you to repentance and renewing your life from the inside out.

- In what way has your practice of lectio divina become "holy ground" for you? What other places or experiences of God in your life have become holy ground?

- Use your imagination to enter the scene of the desert, the mountain, and the fire with Moses. What do you see, hear, smell, taste, and feel? What are you thinking, and what emotions are you experiencing?

- Do you hear God calling you? Respond, "Here I am." What personal message is God offering you in these biblical scenes? What would it take to respond to God with an obedient heart?

- How does Jesus respond to the crowd's idle speculation about the will of God in tragic events? In what ways does his response challenge you to think differently about cause-and-effect speculation in determining the will of God in earthly events?

- What images in the parable of the fig tree challenge you the most? What images offer you comfort?

ORATIO

The fearful possibility of perishing without producing disturbs our hearts and compels us to change. Respond to God's word with repentance and a renewed heart. Begin with these words:

Lord God, I draw near to you with a fascinating attraction and awesome respect. I repent of my injustices and ask you to create a renewed heart within me. Give me the courage to respond to your call and to seek your will through an intimate relationship with you.

Continue praying with a repentant heart and a deep desire for God.

CONTEMPLATIO

⋏

You might want to remove your shoes or sandals as you place yourself under God's loving gaze. Enjoy these holy moments for as long as you wish. Recall and repeat the sacred identity of God, "I AM who AM," to help you remain mindful in God's holy presence.

OPERATIO

⋏

Prayerful reflection on God's word must move us to action. What extra cultivation do you need during Lent in order to bear fruit? What fruit do you want to be producing by the end of this Lent?

Fourth Sunday of Lent

LECTIO

In a comfortable and quiet place of prayer, close off the distractions of the day and enter a moment of stillness. Become aware of your breathing, and ask God's Spirit to fill your heart and guide your listening.

JOSHUA 5:9A, 10-12

The LORD said to Joshua, "Today I have removed the reproach of Egypt from you."

While the Israelites were encamped at Gilgal on the plains of Jericho, they celebrated the Passover on the evening of the fourteenth of the month. On the day after the Passover, they ate of the produce of the land in the form of unleavened cakes and parched grain. On that same day after the Passover, on which they ate of the produce of the land, the manna ceased. No longer was there manna for the Israelites, who that year ate of the yield of the land of Canaan.

The Israelites have recently entered into the land of Canaan, after their exodus from Egypt and their forty-year sojourn in the wilderness. They are now living in the homeland God has promised to their ancestors, the good and prosperous land flowing with milk and honey. The generation that had followed Moses out of

149

Egypt has died, prevented from entering the land because of their faithlessness in the wilderness. But now the new generation, a generation born in the wilderness apart from the bondage of slavery, has come into the promised land.

The wilderness epoch has come to a decisive end. God declares, "Today I have removed the reproach of Egypt from you" (Joshua 5:9). Their slave mentality—the residual stigma of bondage—led to their inability to trust God in the wilderness. But now the shame borne by the Israelites in the wilderness has been taken away by God. The faith of the new generation has overcome the sins of their parents, and now God's people are ready to possess the land. They celebrate the Passover for the first time in their own land. God is sending them no more manna, the bread of the wilderness, but they eat food made from their own produce in the promised land.

Our own Gilgal moments are those times in life when we leave behind a misguided past and begin living a life transformed by hope and confidence. In these graced moments, we are able to leave behind the shameful past of weakness, bondage, and foolish choices, while a new start in faith is made possible through God's forgiveness. In these Gilgal moments, we are able to lay claim to the promises we have been given and possess the life we are called to live. It is truly like discovering our true home or finding it once.

After entering the transforming experience of our ancestors through this sacred text, turn to the gospel parable, another story of homecoming brought about by the gift of forgiveness.

LUKE 15:1-3, 11-32

Tax collectors and sinners were all drawing near to listen to Jesus, but the Pharisees and scribes began to complain, saying, "This man welcomes sinners and eats with them." So to them Jesus addressed this parable: "A man had two sons, and the younger son said to his father, 'Father give me the share of your estate that should come to me.' So the father divided the property between them. After a few days, the younger son collected all his belongings and set off to a distant country where he squandered his inheritance on a life of dissipation. When he had freely spent everything, a severe famine struck that country, and he found himself in dire need. So he hired himself out to one of the local citizens who sent him to his farm to tend the swine. And he longed to eat his fill of the pods on which the swine fed, but nobody gave him any. Coming to his senses he thought, 'How many of my father's hired workers have more than enough food to eat, but here am I, dying from hunger. I shall get up and go to my father and I shall say to him, "Father, I have sinned against heaven and against you. I no longer deserve to be called your son; treat me as you would treat one of your hired workers."' So he got up and went back to his father. While he was still a long way off, his father caught sight of him, and was filled with compassion. He ran to his son, embraced him and kissed him. His son said to him, 'Father, I have sinned against heaven and against you; I no longer deserve to be called your son.' But his father ordered his servants, 'Quickly bring the finest robe and put it on him;

put a ring on his finger and sandals on his feet. Take the fattened calf and slaughter it. Then let us celebrate with a feast, because this son of mine was dead, and has come to life again; he was lost, and has been found.' Then the celebration began. Now the older son had been out in the field and, on his way back, as he neared the house, he heard the sound of music and dancing. He called one of the servants and asked what this might mean. The servant said to him, 'Your brother has returned and your father has slaughtered the fattened calf because he has him back safe and sound.' He became angry, and when he refused to enter the house, his father came out and pleaded with him. He said to his father in reply, 'Look, all these years I served you and not once did I disobey your orders; yet you never gave me even a young goat to feast on with my friends. But when your son returns who swallowed up your property with prostitutes, for him you slaughter the fattened calf.' He said to him, 'My son, you are here with me always; everything I have is yours. But now we must celebrate and rejoice, because your brother was dead and has come to life again; he was lost and has been found.'"

We might best describe this gospel text as the parable of the generous father and his two lost sons. Note that the father divides his property equally between the two sons, keeping nothing for himself. This extraordinary transaction would usually be reserved for the father's death. But instead of responding to his son's request by evicting or shaming him, the father gives everything he has. The father represents the unfathomable grace of God, and the two sons embody the two different attitudes that prevent people from experiencing God's abundance. The younger son is lost in his wasteful lifestyle, and the older son is lost in self-righteousness.

The younger son squanders his inheritance, is reduced to famine, and longs to eat the food of the pigs. Coming to his senses, he prepares a script to deliver to his father, hoping to be accepted back as a hired hand. Like the Israelites in the wilderness who could not escape their slave mentality, the son now thinks of himself as a servant, a sinner, who can never again be accepted as a son. The son makes the first move, turning around and moving toward the father. That's all he needed to do. The father, who had been watching and waiting for him all along, spots him a long way off. He runs to his son, embraces him, and kisses him. The emotion of the joyous father creates a scene of overwhelming love and forgiveness. Though the son seems identified with the stigma of his sin, the father is bent on helping him reverse his shame-filled mind-set. The fine robe, the ring, the sandals, and the feast of veal all proclaim the lost sinner as the father's true son.

The older son has been "out in the field" (Luke 15:25). He is the worker, the one who is responsible and has always done everything his father asked of him. When he hears the music and dancing and realizes his father is celebrating the return of the younger son, he becomes angry and refuses to enter the house. But the father who ran toward one lost son now comes out after the other lost son. The older son complains, "All these years I served you and not once did I disobey your orders" (15:29). He reveals that he, too, has a slave mentality. He does not see himself as a son but as his father's servant who follows his commands. Rather than living the joyful life of a beloved son, he has become a self-pitying victim, filled with bitter resentment.

This parable of Jesus addresses the two groups mentioned at the beginning (Luke 15:1-2). The tax collectors and sinners are mirrored in the attitude of the younger son. The Pharisees and scribes are mirrored in the mind-set of the older son. Yet the parable is addressed to us all. We are all lost children who have been found by our Father. Yet we retain a slave mentality that deprives us of joy in our Father's presence. Either we remain identified with our past sins and cannot accept the fact that we are really sons and daughters, or we follow orders with obedience and can't believe that the Father's love is unmerited and free. Only when we accept our Father's unlimited grace with joy and gratitude can we truly celebrate and feel at home with God.

MEDITATIO

Read the parable of the two lost sons again, pausing to reflect each time that a phrase speaks directly to you. Place yourself in the situation of each son, and consider how you respond to the generous love of the father.

- What prevents you from experiencing and celebrating the abundant love of God? What slave mentality do you see in yourself?

- At Gilgal God removed the reproach of Egypt from his people. When has the experience of God's forgiveness enabled you to leave behind a misguided past and begin a life transformed by hope and confidence?

- We have received abundant gifts from our generous Father, but we often squander those gifts, leading to spiritual famine, when we do not stay in touch with the divine Giver. In what ways do you experience the situation of the younger son in the face of your Father's abundant gifts?

- Sharing in the family of God does not mean following all the commandments with pious precision. When we obey our Father with the mentality of a slave, we become lost sons and daughters. How can the belief that God's love is free and unmerited lead you to experience greater freedom and joy in your Father's home?

- In order to experience the forgiveness of the Father, all we have to do is turn back in the direction of God. We never have to crawl back or make up for our past. When we turn back, then God's love meets us more than halfway. In what way does God want you to turn back to him during this season?

ORATIO

After listening to God through your reading and reflection, respond to God through the words of your prayer. You may wish to begin with these words:

Father of compassionate mercy, I have wandered from your care and have become lost in the slave mentality caused by my sins. I want to turn back to you with all my heart, so that I might experience the joy of living at home with you.

Continue expressing your heart to the Father who knows you intimately, cares about you deeply, and accepts you unconditionally.

CONTEMPLATIO

Imagine the ecstatic joy of the father who spotted his son walking toward him. Place yourself in that scene and savor God's wildly joyful love for you. Let God's love surround and embrace you.

OPERATIO

What would make you feel more at home with God? What Lenten practice would increase the joy you experience as a child of your Father?

Fifth Sunday of Lent

LECTIO

Call upon the renewing Spirit of God as you prepare to read the inspired Scriptures. Open yourself to whatever new insight or encouragement God wishes to offer you.

ISAIAH 43:16-21

Thus says the LORD,
    who opens a way in the sea
    and a path in the mighty waters,
who leads out chariots and horsemen,
    a powerful army,
till they lie prostrate together, never to rise,
    snuffed out and quenched like a wick.
Remember not the events of the past,
    the things of long ago consider not;
see, I am doing something new!
    Now it springs forth, do you not perceive it?
In the desert I make a way,
    in the wasteland, rivers.
Wild beasts honor me,
    jackals and ostriches,
for I put water in the desert
    and rivers in the wasteland

for my chosen people to drink,
    the people whom I formed for myself,
       that they might announce my praise.

God is constantly calling his people to new beginnings. "See, I am doing something new!" (Isaiah 43:19) is the ever-present stance of God at work among us. God is not just the deity of past history; God is Lord of the past, present, and future. Our challenge is to always be expectant and ready for the new redemptive action of God in the world.

This song of Isaiah looks back to God's saving work, beginning with his enslaved people in Egypt. Those extraordinary events of liberation set the pattern for God's work throughout the centuries of Israel's covenanted relationship with him. From the memory of God's former manifestations, the prophet calls the people to discern God's actions in the present moment and to look toward the glorious future he has promised.

The prophet is addressing the exiles in Babylon, preparing them for a new exodus as God frees his people from Babylonian captivity. God will guide Israel across a new desert and bring them back to the land promised to them. Years later Jews, and then Christians, would understand these words of Isaiah to speak about the messianic times. Jesus is the new Moses who will lead his people to redemption through "his exodus that he was going to accomplish in Jerusalem" (Luke 9:31).

As disciples of Jesus, we are children of a dynamic God, not just a God of the past. We can look back at all those remarkable events of past ages, but those wonderful works have not come to an end. We can encounter God just as powerfully and much more personally than could our ancient ancestors in Israel. God is acting today: "See, I am doing something new! / Now it springs forth, do you not perceive it?" (Isaiah 43:19).

Realizing that the Scriptures always proclaim God's new beginnings, read this familiar passage from John's Gospel as if for the first time. Expect to hear God's voice anew, and prepare to be challenged by the powerful words and deeds of Jesus.

JOHN 8:1-11

Jesus went to the Mount of Olives. But early in the morning he arrived again in the temple area, and all the people started coming to him, and he sat down and taught them. Then the scribes and the Pharisees brought a woman who had been caught in adultery and made her stand in the middle. They said to him, "Teacher, this woman was caught in the very act of committing adultery. Now in the law, Moses commanded us to stone such women. So what do you say?" They said this to test him, so that they could have some charge to bring against him. Jesus bent down and began to write on the ground with his finger. But when they continued asking him, he straightened up and said to them, "Let the one among you who is without sin be the first to throw a stone at her." Again he bent down and wrote on the ground. And in response, they went away one by one, beginning with the elders. So he was left alone with the woman before him. Then Jesus straightened up and said to her, "Woman, where are they? Has no one condemned you?" She replied, "No one, sir." Then Jesus said, "Neither do I condemn you. Go, and from now on do not sin any more."

Though commentary on this scene usually focuses on the woman and her sin, the gospel writer is equally concerned with the men and their judgmental approach. The response of Jesus is described in two parallel scenes, each beginning when Jesus bends down and writes on the grounds. Each time that he rises from the ground, he pronounces a pivotal verse of the narrative. He speaks first to the scribes and Pharisees about sin, and then to the woman about sin.

The woman's accusers state that she has been "caught in the very act of committing adultery" (John 8:4). The religious authorities clearly have no real concern for the fate of this woman. They are out to get Jesus. Neither do they care about the injured husband or the partner in adultery, who has apparently gotten off scot-free. The law of Moses, to which the accusers refer, prescribes death by stoning for both the man and the woman involved (Leviticus 20:10; Deuteronomy 22:22-24). They are testing Jesus in order to trap him in a conflict with the Torah of Israel.

In the midst of this awkward scene, Jesus responds calmly and tenderly. His first response is nonverbal; he bends down and writes with his finger on the ground. If nothing else can be made of this gesture, at least it buys time for reflection and separates Jesus from the zealous fervor of the woman's accusers. By lowering himself to the ground, Jesus physically distinguishes his position from theirs.

With tranquil confidence, in contrast to the pressurized hysteria of the scene, Jesus stands up and states, "Let the one among you who is without sin be the first to throw a stone at her" (John 8:7).

The mob is disarmed. The accusers become the accused. They are forced to direct their gaze inwardly, where they are able to discern whether or not they are in a position to condemn the woman. To their credit, not one of them exempts himself from self-judgment and throws the first stone at her. As Jesus again stoops to the grounds and writes in the dirt, his opponents gradually walk away. Though they had arrived on the scene as an undifferentiated rabble, they go away "one by one" (8:8), as individuals who have become more aware of their inner selves through their encounter with Jesus.

Jesus is left alone with the woman. He again rises from the ground and speaks, this time to her. He is the first person to address her directly in the narrative. The forgiveness of Jesus gives her the opportunity to live her life anew. Not only has Jesus saved her physical life from those who would stone her, but he also refuses to let her be defined by the guilt of past sin and directs her toward a life of freedom with an open future in relationship to God.

In this parallel narrative, Jesus addresses the religious authorities, inviting them to be healed of their judgmental spirit, as well as the victimized woman, inviting her to be healed from the sin of adultery. Rather than saying sin is unimportant, Jesus shows that it is too important for mere humans to arbitrate. Jesus has taught that God did not send his Son into the world to "condemn" but that the world might be "saved" (John 3:17). He wants us to be freed from our past and to experience God's transforming grace.

MEDITATIO

⋀

- In what way is the reading from Isaiah a song of new beginnings? How do you hear the voice of God, "See, I am doing something new," directed at your own life?

- How is the gospel scene also a story of new beginnings? How does it offer you a new way of looking at God's dealing with sin?

- Since this scene is the only one in the Bible in which Jesus is presented as writing, commentators have offered lots of speculation about the meaning of this action. Some have suggested that Jesus is indicating that our sins are registered in sand and can be wiped away with repentance and forgiveness. How does this explanation encourage you?

- Others have suggested that Jesus is simply doodling in the dust, pointing out that we are formed from dust and to dust we will return (see Genesis 3:19). In view of the gospel scene, why would Jesus want to make this point?

- What would it take for you to put down the stone of judgment? How does cultivating your ability to see yourself as a sinner enable you to extend yourself in compassion to others?

ORATIO

⅄

Respond to God's word with your own words of prayer. Include the ideas, images, and vocabulary of Scripture to enrich the content of your prayer. Use this prayer for a starter:

Just and merciful Lord, you forgave the adulterous woman and the judgmental men. Help me to realize the depths of my sin and the liberation you offer me through your forgiveness. Continue to transform my life with your healing grace.

Continue to pray as your heart directs you.

CONTEMPLATIO

⅄

Be still before God, conscious of your sin and open to the way God wants to transform you. Let God move your heart with compassion for yourself and others.

OPERATIO

⅄

God says to you, "See, I am doing something new!" What new thing do you wish God to accomplish in your life this week? What do you need to do to open your life to God's renewing Spirit?

Palm Sunday of the Lord's Passion

LECTIO

Place a crucifix, cross, or palm branch before you to help you focus on the Lord's passion and death. Ask the Holy Spirit to help you listen and respond to the *sacra pagina* as you reflect on the texts for the beginning of this Holy Week.

When you have quieted your external and internal distractions, dedicate this time for sacred conversation with God.

ISAIAH 50:4-7

The Lord GOD has given me
    a well-trained tongue,
that I might know how to speak to the weary
    a word that will rouse them.
Morning after morning
    he opens my ear that I may hear;
and I have not rebelled,
    have not turned back.
I gave my back to those who beat me,
    my cheeks to those who plucked my beard;
my face I did not shield
    from buffets and spitting.

The Lord GOD is my help,
　　therefore I am not disgraced;
I have set my face like flint,
　　knowing that I shall not be put to shame.

As the church gathers to proclaim the Passion of Jesus Christ during Holy Week, we also hear the words of the Servant Songs of Isaiah (42:1-9; 49:1-7; 50:4-11; 52:13–53:12). On Palm Sunday, as the Passion is proclaimed from Matthew, Mark, or Luke, we hear this third Servant Song, and on Good Friday, as the Passion from John's Gospel is proclaimed, we listen to the fourth of the Servant Songs. These Servant texts have profoundly shaped the church's understanding of Jesus, and they find their fullest meaning in his suffering and death. Like Jesus, the Servant is beaten, spat upon, struck in the face, and persecuted for carrying out his divinely appointed mission.

Though God's Servant is treated disgracefully, he says, "I am not disgraced" (Isaiah 50:7). He suffers insults and beating without receiving them internally. He does not lose his honor and is not put to shame because God is his help and strength. His persecutors may take his life, but they cannot destroy who he is. Though the humiliation inflicted upon him is real enough, it fails in its purpose. God's Servant knows that in reality, he is the victor.

The key to the Servant's strength and endurance is his attention to God's word. Morning after morning he listens, and then his life becomes a proclamation. He internalizes God's word; the word becomes flesh within him. He know "how to speak to the weary" (Isaiah 50:4) because he speaks God's word with his lips and especially with his life.

Motivated by God's inspired prophet to internalize the word of God, prepare to listen and receive within you the Passion of our Lord Jesus Christ according to Luke.

LUKE 23:1-49

The elders of the people and chief priests and scribes arose and brought Jesus before Pilate. They brought charges against him, saying, "We found this man misleading our people; he opposes the payment of taxes to Caesar and maintains that he is the Christ, a king." Pilate asked him, "Are you the king of the Jews?" He said to him in reply, "You say so." Pilate then addressed the chief priests and the crowds, "I find this man not guilty." But they were adamant and said, "He is inciting the people with his teaching throughout all Judea, from Galilee where he began even to here."

On hearing this Pilate asked if the man was a Galilean; and upon learning that he was under Herod's jurisdiction, he sent him to Herod who was in Jerusalem at that time. Herod was very glad to see Jesus; he had been wanting to see him for a long time, for he had heard about him and had been hoping to see him perform some sign. He questioned him at length, but he gave him no answer. The chief priests and scribes, meanwhile, stood by accusing him harshly. Herod and his soldiers treated him contemptuously and mocked him, and after clothing him in resplendent garb, he sent him back to Pilate. Herod and Pilate became friends that very day, even though they had been enemies formerly. Pilate then summoned the chief priests, the rulers, and the people and said to them, "You brought this man to me and accused him of inciting the people to revolt. I have conducted my investigation in your presence and have not found this man guilty of the charges you have brought against him, nor did Herod, for he sent him back to us. So no capital crime has been committed by him. Therefore I shall have him flogged and then release him."

But all together they shouted out, "Away with this man! Release Barabbas to us."—Now Barabbas had been imprisoned for a rebellion that had taken place in the city and for murder.—Again Pilate addressed them, still wishing to release Jesus, but they continued their shouting, "Crucify him! Crucify him!" Pilate addressed them a third time, "What evil has this man done? I found him guilty of no capital crime. Therefore I shall have him flogged and then release him." With loud shouts, however, they persisted in calling for his crucifixion, and their voices prevailed. The verdict of Pilate was that their demand should be granted. So he released the man who had been imprisoned for rebellion and murder, for whom they asked, and he handed Jesus over to them to deal with as they wished.

As they led him away they took hold of a certain Simon, a Cyrenian, who was coming in from the country; and after laying the cross on him, they made him carry it behind Jesus. A large crowd of people followed Jesus, including many women who mourned and lamented him. Jesus turned to them and said, "Daughters of Jerusalem, do not weep for me;

weep instead for yourselves and for your children for indeed, the days are coming when people will say, 'Blessed are the barren, the wombs that never bore and the breasts that never nursed.' At that time people will say to the mountains, 'Fall upon us!' and to the hills, 'Cover us!' for if these things are done when the wood is green what will happen when it is dry?" Now two others, both criminals, were led away with him to be executed.

When they came to the place called the Skull, they crucified him and the criminals there, one on his right, the other on his left. Then Jesus said, "Father, forgive them, they know not what they do." They divided his garments by casting lots. The people stood by and watched; the rulers, meanwhile, sneered at him and said, "He saved others, let him save himself if he is the chosen one, the Christ of God." Even the soldiers jeered at him. As they approached to offer him wine they called out, "If you are King of the Jews, save yourself." Above him there was an inscription that read, "This is the King of the Jews."

Now one of the criminals hanging there reviled Jesus, saying, "Are you not the Christ? Save yourself and us." The other, however, rebuking him, said in reply, "Have you no fear of God, for you are subject to the same condemnation? And indeed, we have been condemned justly, for the sentence we received corresponds to our crimes, but this man has done nothing criminal." Then he said, "Jesus, remember me when you come into your kingdom." He replied to him, "Amen, I say to you, today you will be with me in Paradise."

It was now about noon and darkness came over the whole land until three in the afternoon because of an eclipse of the sun. Then the veil of the temple was torn down the middle. Jesus cried out in a loud voice, "Father, into your hands I commend my spirit"; and when he had said this he breathed his last.

[Here all kneel and pause for a short time.]

The centurion who witnessed what had happened glorified God and said, "This man was innocent beyond doubt." When all the people who had gathered for this spectacle saw what had happened, they returned home beating their breasts; but all his acquaintances stood at a distance, including the women who had followed him from Galilee and saw these events.

In a scene unique to Luke's Passion account, Jesus meets the women of Jerusalem and tells them not to weep for him but for themselves and their children. For the Passion is not just the sad story of Jesus. It is, rather, a story of divine nobility, passionate love, steadfast courage, and unlimited forgiveness. The cross is the great intersection between divine goodness and human helplessness, in which God becomes vulnerable and humanity becomes strong. The real sadness is not the suffering of Jesus; it is the tragedy of human sin and the destruction it inflicts upon the world.

In another detail found only in Luke's narrative, Jesus asks God to forgive his torturers. As he is nailed to the cross, in a remarkable expression of compassion, Jesus says, "Father, forgive them, they know not what they do" (Luke 23:34). For those of us who find it next to impossible to imitate Jesus' tremendous example of love, it is helpful to note that Jesus' statement is a prayer. Whether or not Jesus was humanly ready to forgive, he prayed for his persecutors as an expression of love of enemies. When we are confronted with the challenge of forgiving unrepentant adversaries, we can turn to the prayer of Jesus on the cross. What may not come spontaneously from the human heart can be requested in prayer.

Luke's Passion is also the only version to compare the responses of the two criminals crucified beside Jesus. While one joins in the mockery of the crowds, the other repents on the cross. First, the repentant criminal acknowledges his sins, admitting that he has been condemned justly and deserves punishment for his deeds. Then he turns to Jesus for help: "Jesus, remember me when you come into your kingdom" (Luke 23:42). The sinner calls on the name of Jesus, recognizing that in his death, Jesus is the source of his salvation. The repentant criminal receives salvation from Jesus without hesitation: "Today you will be with me in Paradise" (23:43). Jesus, the one who came "to seek and to save what was lost" (19:10), continued to welcome the outcast and the sinner until his final breath. Jesus died as he had lived, extending his saving mercy to all.

MEDITATIO

Just as God prepared his Servant for the word, God has opened your ears that you might hear, and you have heard with the ears of your heart. Now seek to assimilate these texts in all their depth so that you can respond to them with your life as you journey through this Holy Week.

- How is it possible not to be disgraced and suffer shame when you are mistreated or humiliated by others? What modern-day prophets embody this mind-set of God's Servant?

- We can tell much about the unique emphasis of each evangelist by comparing the texts of the three synoptic gospels side by side. What does the Passion according to Luke seem to especially emphasize about Jesus?

- Though our usual Holy Week liturgies focus on the solitary cross of Jesus, occasionally we are reminded that there were three crosses on Calvary. What do you want to remember the next time you see the image of the three crosses? How do they remind you of your relationship to the crucified Savior?

- What does the repentant criminal teach you about the process of conversion? What do you want to imitate as you draw close to the crucified Jesus this week?

- As we age, there are many things in life for which it becomes too late. But it is never too late to turn over one's life to Jesus Christ. How do you feel about people who turn to Christ in the final hours of life? What do you believe about their salvation?

ORATIO

In Luke's account, the final cry of Jesus from the cross is from Psalm 31. Speak or chant the words of this psalm as a prayerful response to God's word.

You, O Lord, are my rock and my fortress; for your name's sake you will lead and guide me. You will free me from the snare they set for me, for you are my refuge. Into your hands I commend my spirit; you will redeem me, O Lord, O faithful God.

Continue to pray in your own words, seeking to imitate Jesus' complete trust in the Father.

CONTEMPLATIO

Spend some moments in silence, uniting your heart with the trust and confidence of Jesus. Slowly repeat the phrase "Father, into your hands I commend my spirit."

OPERATIO

As you enter the church's most holy week, determine to follow Jesus on his journey to the cross so that you might experience the joy of his resurrection. Join with the church's liturgical rituals so that Christ's paschal mystery may be present to you in all its saving power.

Calendar of Sunday Lectionary Cycles

The lectionary cycle for the Sunday liturgical readings begins each year on the First Sunday of Advent and ends each year on the last Sunday of Ordinary Time, which is the Solemnity of Christ the King. Here are the cycles that will be used by the church through 2019.

Advent 2009 to Christ the King 2010: Year C

Advent 2010 to Christ the King 2011: Year A

Advent 2011 to Christ the King 2012: Year B

Advent 2012 to Christ the King 2013: Year C

Advent 2013 to Christ the King 2014: Year A

Advent 2014 to Christ the King 2015: Year B

Advent 2015 to Christ the King 2016: Year C

Advent 2016 to Christ the King 2017: Year A

Advent 2017 to Christ the King 2018: Year B

Advent 2018 to Christ the King 2019: Year C